The Team
A Mother's Wisdom from the Other Side

BOOK ONE
by
CRYSTAL "TEDDY" KEY
As Communicated to Frances Rae Key

Dedicated with great love to Teddy's and Frances'
daughters, grandchildren and great-grandchildren:

Kelly Elizabeth
Wendy Aura
Autumn Maria
Julia Rae
Meghan Elizabeth
Julian Tosh
Morgan Sky
Gene Luke
Sydney Crystal
Sophia Frances
Madison Brooke

And in memory of
Raymond Key
Vivien Ferry

And to all our Teammates,
here and beyond…

Deepest gratitude to Oscar Senn for designing the covers for the Team Book Series. The photographs used on the covers were taken at Teddy Key's home where a circular garden with angel statues has been created. On October 26, 2013, huge white spheres and beams of light appeared on the statues, which Frances captured on camera. Two of these pictures are used on the covers of Books 2 and 3. The covers of Books 1 and 4 feature angel statue photos without spheres, taken on a different day. All the sphere photos are available for viewing at www.TheTeamBooks.com.

THE INSIGHTS

INTRODUCTION

This is the first book of a four-book series. The books were written over a three-year period and gradually released in 2011, 2012, 2013, and 2017. In this first book, the insights fundamental to the series are given. In subsequent books, each insight is intensely expanded. It is generally recognized that this first book is communicated primarily by Teddy Key and that a wider group of Teammates offer their wisdom in the following books, yielding a wide variety of writing styles and types of information as the series progresses. Two chapters from Book 2 have been moved into this book, "True Joy" and "An Experimental Approach." Please note the words "he" and "she" are used randomly throughout the books.

Dear Reader,

On October 9, 2010, at 4:15 am, my beloved mother, Teddy Key, passed away at her home from cancer. My sister Kelly, my daughter Julie, and my sister's boyfriend, Alan, and I held her in our arms throughout the last hours of her life. We prayed over her, anointed her body with oil and wept profusely as we said goodbye to the body that had housed a very great and wise soul for eighty-six years. We knew how much we would miss her unconditional love, her feisty energy, and her forgiving heart. While we were relieved that she was free from a body that no longer served her, we felt keenly the loss of the true leader of our family — our spiritual teacher, our mother, grandmother, and friend — and we entered into a state of grief.

Just a few weeks later, Teddy let us know she hadn't gone far, and that she had much more to teach us. She began to communicate with me telepathically and through automatic writing about her insights from the Other Side. The rush of information was so intense that within only three weeks, the collection of writings you are holding in your hands was complete.

These insights are not from me; nor are they intended for me alone. The sheer volume of what is being offered is astounding; the inpouring of unique concepts, analogies, and descriptions and the pace at which they appear is astonishing to me. Although I have edited some of the grammar and have put the chapters in a sequence that seems more logical, for the most part the material is verbatim.

Many people have asked me to describe what it was like to receive a book like this — what I actually heard, how I felt, and so forth. I will try my best to explain the process as I experienced it, although I have to say at the outset, it is hard to explain the inexplicable. I first heard Mother's voice ringing through me and around me in answer to questions that I was thinking about while traveling on a plane to visit two of my daughters who lived in New York City. It had been just nineteen days since she had died, and as I gazed across the glorious sky, the pain of her absence, followed by the joy of her presence, enveloped me. The voice was startlingly clear and unmistakably hers. She gave no preface to her statements, and simply started talking to me as if we were in the middle of a conversation.

The experience of hearing her voice can best be compared to what it's like when you hear a song in your head — the music, lead singer, backup singers, lyrics and all. Rarely do we question how music flows through our minds in such a way-in fact; it's a common event for most people. I can only say that in the same manner, Mother's voice sounded as real and felt as natural to me as it had when she was alive.

At first, I felt I was having a personal conversation with her, and we talked about some things pertinent to my own life. Then the topics branched off into more universal themes. I was not alarmed or frightened — in fact I was thrilled, comforted and excited. I had no doubt of its authenticity. Looking back, I suppose I thought that it would be a one-time encounter on the plane that would end when we landed. I didn't really analyze it too much at the time, but simply wrote down what I was hearing so I wouldn't lose the treasure I knew I was being given. As you can see from the amount of text in this book, it wasn't to be a one-time encounter. For many months I was bombarded with a series of conceptual realizations, which were accompanied by Mother's voice giving detailed explanations, examples, analogies, methods, affirmations and prayers.

Most of the information came unbidden, flooding my being when I was otherwise occupied or in a relaxed state of mind rather than when I deliberately tried to seek it. In fact, on the rare occasion I attempted to induce it, I rarely received anything. I soon realized that I needed to carry a notepad around with me so I could be ready to write down what I was hearing, for I found that if I didn't respond immediately, I would usually have no memory of what had been said, or at best just a vague notion of the concept with no substantial accompanying details. I also found that the best way for me to record it was to write it out by hand. Then it would come in a great rush, as if it had a mind of its own, much sloppier and larger than my own writing, but more accurate. A few times I tried using a tape recorder or typing on a computer, but the handwriting proved to be the strongest medium by far.

The inspiration always began with Mother's voice, but sometimes it would shift and the concepts would be impressed upon my mind in a flash, as if I'd seen a whole movie in a split second and knew the intricacies of the entire plot. Then, I would take this concentrated kernel of information and listen for her embellishments and examples so the concept could be fully fleshed out. Perhaps you have felt this before when you were suddenly struck with a profound understanding about something and just *knew* the complete story behind a certain situation or topic. Maybe it took just an instant of time, but in that instant was compressed a

11

monumental degree of comprehension about a subject. Perhaps you felt you were being "hit between the eyes" with a single concept or even a whole set of principles, and afterwards you couldn't believe that you hadn't grasped before what was now so obvious, clear and simple. This is the manner in which much of this book was received.

For example, when I wrote ,"The Hodgepodge that is the Earth," I was standing in a flea market! Suddenly, the voice began, and I felt such a wave of understanding about what each of those little buttons and bows represented that I actually felt weak for a moment. Out came the notepad and what I consider to be one of the most quirky and fascinating chapters in the book came gushing forth, my hand hastily trying to keep up with the rapid-fire "download".

What surprised and actually entertained me as I wrote Mother's words were the bright, unusual phrases she chose. In addition, although some of the basic concepts she talked about are familiar to me, there were just as many that I could never have dreamed of, had never heard of, and certainly had never looked at from that particular point of view. They puzzled and astounded me even as they appeared on the page before me. I often laughed to myself as I wrote, amazed at how apropos were the analogies she used, and how original and fresh was her perspective.

Because Mother was a teacher by profession, she used examples involving children and educational practices as her primary theme. I can't tell you how many people who have read the books have said, "That's your mother all right. It sounds just like her," for Mother had a somewhat formal way of speaking due to her Australian heritage, and her conversation was always peppered with humorous sayings.

Another part of the experience is something I've hesitated to talk about, but feel that it's important to describe. Since about the age of 20, I've had the occasional, but rare, experience of feeling a warm, tingling sensation in the center of my forehead when I pray, mediate, or have any kind of intense spiritual insight. During the weeks that this book was written, that tingling sensation, always very pleasant and relaxing, was there most of the time. It was sometimes faint and at other times so strong it was hard to keep my eyes open. I know there are many far-fetched descriptions of the "third eye" of spiritual awakening out there, and I am reluctant to associate what I have felt with those kinds of descriptions. I can only say that for me it was an actual physical sensation accompanied by a level of supernatural intuition, and has become a signal to me of the purity of the information given and connection I have with my spiritual Teammates.

I used this sensation as a barometer of sorts, for I noticed that when I wrote the material, if my energy or sense of direct connection waned because of fatigue or lack of focus, the sensation would fade as well. I recognized that fading away as a signal that I wasn't perfectly on track with something, so when that happened I would rest a while, then go back and re-read what I'd been working on. I could always tell if what I'd written hadn't captured the message adequately. It would read to me like "filler" compared to the other material, and I would wait until that sensation returned full force, and Mother's voice clarified how to correct it. These "corrections" never concerned the actual concepts in the information, but were more about the choice of some of the words themselves. The extreme care that was taken with how the material was worded made it very clear to me that the *choice of specific words and phrases* was vitally important to the whole process. I came to see that the weaving together of certain words unleashed a certain kind of energy, emotion or vibration that other word choices did not generate.

I came to understand that these words and the images they conjured up were pieced together as they were for a very precise purpose, much as the color and design of a tapestry is woven according to a certain code or formula that determines the quality and symbolic value of its final appearance. While the inflow of all this information was a very intuitive and organic process, at times it also felt very "mathematical" to me, as if various parts were being assembled in accordance with a pre-ordained blueprint. I have learned through this experience that when conditions are right and a certain level of openness and trust exists, spiritual Team members can and will break the bonds of what is considered "normal" human experience to bring forth something they know it is time to divulge. As Mother teasingly put it to me, they know "how to make hay while the sun shines!" In keeping with her usual playful attitude, she also said at one time, "Isn't this *fun?*" Truly, joy is Mother's trademark, and I felt that joy and an incredibly brilliant kind of energy all throughout the time I was writing these books.

Certainly everyone who knows my life is aware that I have "feet of clay" and that these beautiful teachings are lessons for me just as they are for anyone else, lessons I aspire to but cannot claim mastery of. When I read these books, I feel I'm reading something written by somebody else...because I am. My hope is that these insights will do for you what they have done for me: give you new eyes through which you may view all aspects of your life, while linking you more and more intimately with your spiritual legacy, your own Team and its mission. May your Mind be receptive, your Heart tender, and your Soul expansive as you encounter Teddy's Team in the form of these extremely valuable insights...

Sincerely,
Frances Key
January, 2011

OPENING
October 28, 2010

You are not alone. You're not really even functioning as one person. Nobody is. For you are a member of a Team, a spiritual Team, as close to you as breathing… and I am a part of your Team.

I speak to your soul as your Team member, to your heart as your Mother, and to your mind as your teacher and friend. We are so fortunate to have so many layers of connection to each other, making this work so natural and simple for us. I want to tell you of where I am… it is a place that you will recognize from my description, for you have spent more time here than on Earth. It is the familiar tree house upon the mountaintop that you've always seen in your mind; a candle burns in the window there, waiting for you.

The Universe is composed of everlasting bands of Light, which are filled with countless points of consciousness within each band. Indeed, there is no end to the stretch of Light in evolution, and all these components combine as the Absolute, which is also called by the warm and familiar word, God. As one who stands upon a glorious mountain peak wants to cry out with awe into the vastness, so am I bursting with a yearning to convey what it is I now can see. Yet I know that while these vast concepts are enthralling, the most useful concepts for you, right now upon the Earth, are that of your spiritual connection to your Team, how your physical body relates to your spiritual body, methods for accelerating your development, tools to dispel negativity, and the overriding mission of life on Earth.

It's "All Hands on Deck!" for the world right now, and one of the reasons I'm able to do this with you is because of that fact. Teams are escalating their work, bringing many things to full fruition, to prepare for a major "overhaul" in a sense. These points of monumental change and revelation occur many times throughout the cycles upon the Earth. We are all positioned perfectly for what is to come. From here, it is a light show. Vibrations of great contrast are pulsating across the Earth in massive sheets of color, energy and power. There is so much varied intention swirling all around humanity, it would be impossible for things to stay the same. Our Team, like all teams, is well aware of what is needed and how to maximize what we have to offer.

This is but one of the reasons I am reaching out to you. The other reasons are that my enduring love for all of you is so great, and our Team so invested in you, and my personal connection to you so profound, it is impossible to deny the impulse to do all I can to enlighten your journey. Be assured, I am still walking with all of you.

All along the spectrum of spiritual development there are various groupings of souls who work together for a wide variety of purposes; some for general reasons, others for very definite purposes. Great efforts are made to make very specific plans when it is clear to a Team that certain events, places, and rendezvous are necessary to facilitate the most efficient and beneficial connections for the progress of everyone involved. This is one of those times.

But it isn't the details of the "assignment" at hand which are the greatest concern. Rather, it is the acceleration of vibrations that is so important, both the electrifying, shooting-star type bursts of vibration that occur during moments of sudden upliftment, as well as the steady hum of the consistently offered vibration of stability. Nothing is as important as the vibration of intention that each of you is emanating from deep within your being, for this and only this is what is felt, seen, sensed, absorbed, used, and redirected by your Team. Outer circumstances are immaterial when compared to the importance of one's vibratory quality.

Plans are made by the Team, but plans are often changed without a loss of achievement as long as the vibratory offering is somehow generated and directed elsewhere. Therefore, the overarching assignment remains the establishment of a certain assemblage of energies, consisting of every Team member's contribution, including those upon the Earth and those working from other dimensions. For this reason, *you are never operating solo.* On the contrary, you are a representative, as it were, of your Team, and they are filtering information to you as you are filtering your impressions and activities back to them. This is a constant flow, never stopping under any circumstance. It can, however, be brought to a dense trickle through one's stubborn embrace of illusion or outright rejection of the connection. Conversely, it can become a constant, pulsating current if you are ready and willing to join forces with it.

Imagine a representative of a company being sent out to a conference. His head is full of facts and figures, concrete goals and mile-high dreams, some of them confidential and some that he is ready to make known. He has a mission to accomplish, and the hopes of the business are riding on him. His supervisors and co-workers have prepared him, and he has learned his lessons well. He has weaknesses, too, which both he and the others are well aware of. This is taken into account when he is sent on assignment; nonetheless, his talents and capacity to grow into fulfilling a greater role make him useful to the whole.

Before and after the conference, he is in touch with the Team, but when he stands up to deliver his material to the audience, it's up to him to be the strongest representative he can be, transmitting what he's been taught to the best of his ability. Their words echo in his mind, their faces are before him, and the notes that they helped him to prepare are in his hands. More influential than anything he has to say, however, is the *force of authenticity* he brings to the presentation… that indescribable quality that can make or break the "deal". After leaving the conference, he returns to his place of origin filled with information about what was well received and what was not, where he erred and where he excelled, and it is this information that enables the Team to regroup and plan anew.

This analogy, business or otherwise, reflects the basic structure of how souls unite into teams for a variety of missions, in order that every member may grow and expand. It also reflects the fact that every member, at some time or another, bears the weight for the rest of their Team, willingly accepting challenges that belong to the group in order that some members can be freed up to complete a part of the mission. They may choose to act as a placeholder in a sense, or a maintainer of some kind of foundation so the others may climb. Is this not so within any family unit or other earthly organization? Love on all levels, whether spiritual or physical, leads one to sacrifice in support of others.

I am here to tell you that you are valued, honored, and needed by your Team. And I am here to tell you that by remembering who you are, the Team to whom you belong, and the legacy that you carry within your spiritual DNA, you can transform your entire existence.

DISTANCE

"Mom, is there any distance for you?"
This question, tearfully directed to my mother as I looked across the sky from the window of the plane I was traveling in, was not one I really expected an answer to. However, when I heard her beautiful Australian accent ringing in my ears, my tears vanished. As if we were sitting side by side in that plane, she quite casually said, "Not the way it is for you, no. Not in a Time/Space kind of way, only in an Expansion of intention kind of way. My distance is more like the scope of my intentions." As the fascinating explanation continued, I took paper and pen and began to write what I heard her say. Little did I know that the writings would continue daily, many hours a day, for about three weeks, not stopping until she said, "That's Book One!" It would then resume, producing a series of books.

She explained further:
The concept of your distance is equivalent to me casting a ray of intention like a fisherman casts a line. As my sense of casting improves, my delight in hitting the target improves, too. In your denser realm you have "here, there, and in between." In this realm we have "here, here, and here". Our intention determines the "here" we are focused upon, but all the alternative possibilities are available as we wish. You are doing something similar right now. You're sitting in this plane, aware there are many other people here as well, but you aren't directing any attention whatsoever towards them. The sky is visible out of the corner of your right eye, the flowers on someone's dress out of the corner of your other eye, and you steadily maintain a vague awareness of all this. There are many other things you are aware of too, *but you are simply choosing not to react to them.* You also know that in a flash, you could switch gears and make any one of them the object of your full attention and thereby interact with them, if you wanted to do so.

So it is for me regarding distance. A shift of focus and I am instantly there. I can drop into the place where someone abides, an individual's "home of consciousness" so to speak, like you drop into a certain neighborhood to visit someone. What is so delightful here on the Other Side is that each person resides at the highest point of which they're capable, and so they are completely fulfilled and happy. They know there are infinite levels beyond them, but they also know that they are exactly where they best belong. As a result, the vibration of bliss is everywhere.

My ability to gather in multiple layers of experience and information all at once is hard to describe. While focused on you, I am able to remain aware of my other surroundings. But not only that - I'm aware of all the possibilities beyond my immediate surroundings. These vast possibilities do not overwhelm or confuse me as they would you. Rather, they invigorate and inspire me, filling me up rather than scattering or depleting my energy. Such a freedom it is to have awareness of all possibilities and the power to instantly create any one of them by changing my focus. It's not my personal power, though. It's the power of the underpinnings of Universal Law operating in its rawest form that makes all this possible.

You see, Universal Law passes through a filter before manifesting on Earth. This filter adjusts these laws to the vibratory level available in your dimension. It is elongated in a way, rather like taking a piece of putty in its natural state and stretching it into a new shape. This elongation causes Universal Law to take on a recognizable form so you may experience it as Time, Space, Distance and all the "here's and there's" that you need to function. It's a wonderful thing to watch, this stretching, molding and settling down of things so they can be used upon the earth.

It is much like how you prepare a child's environment when you go to teach him something. You might remove any distractions from his reach, lay out certain items in a special order, or any number of things to manipulate what is presented to him so he gets the most out of the lesson. So it is on the Earth plane, where events are laid out in sequence to demonstrate cause and effect more clearly.

Any distance you associate with me is a product of your ingenious, yet limited, human brain, which needs to think in a manner that is based upon Time and Space so you can function there. I'm not visible to you because I'm no longer using that particular body, but a portion of me is with you, and an element of my focus is still upon you just as you are retaining a portion of awareness of everything that's around you in this plane even while you're communicating with me.

There are others here, too, that want to teach you. They're all members of our spiritual Team. Remember them? I know you will, for they are always with you.

THE POWER OF THOUGHTS
AND MEMORY MAGNETS

Teams have many tools and methods available to them as they fulfill their missions, and while the form of these tools may take on different shapes depending on the dimension a soul is using, the principles behind those tools are the same. On the Earth, your primary tools for the completion of a mission are your thoughts, which produce words (written and spoken) and actions, the visions and sounds you create through the arts, and the design of useful and inspirational objects.

The influences of these elements take place both in Time and out of Time. In other words, these creations can be slowly distributed and received throughout the Earth through the usual channels (in Time), even while they are sending forth ripples of energy far out into the realm of ideation from the moment they are imagined (out of Time). Bear in mind that everything out of Time is happening in split seconds, according to the speed of thought, so the root intention that underlies any thought is launched simultaneously.

This is why your "little bit" matters so very much! The impetus behind your thoughts, words, songs, paintings, and other creations do not stay "little". They grow, lengthen, widen, stretch, and magnify at a rate of which you can't conceive. Every burst of intention and thought radiates out and is duplicated as it flows, replicating itself throughout eternity. Like clusters of cells which multiply to form a child in the womb, so do your emanations multiply, link, and endure. Every second, hour, day, week, year, and forevermore, your thoughts, which some may consider so insignificant, are growing by leaps and bounds as they seek out and merge with the thoughts of others that are of like kind. For this reason, your Team is constantly pouring powerfully enriched intentions of all kinds towards you. And for this same reason, all spiritual teachers throughout the centuries have beseeched humanity to elevate their thoughts, for this is where everything else germinates.

It is easy to see, then, how any emanations of loving-kindness that you offer are such a treasure for your Team, for they enter the hearts of other people throughout the world and are matched by thoughts of equivalent proportion and quality, yielding tremendous influences far beyond your sight or awareness. These match-ups generate a sweeping impetus that determines the speed and size of these combinations of thoughts, like a rapidly growing snowball hurtling down a never-ending slope. In this way these emanations are leveraged, like a person in business who knows how to invest a few cents to yield a million dollars. If only everyone could realize this fact... that with every breath and every beat of your heart, you are creating *something* that extends into the vastness of the Universe that will be duplicated endlessly and will live forever. In truth, you cannot *not* create, for it is the fundamental nature of both your body and soul to do so. Therefore, if we must continuously create, let us agree to create with the purest intentions we can muster.

To accomplish this, you must acknowledge that your negative emanations, once released into the ether, also have a life that is expanding. However, even as you face this reality, take heart in the fact that you have an antidote to this quandary. The formula is simple... double your positive projections to neutralize a negative projection. You have the power within yourself to be an instrument for such neutralization, and oh, what a tremendous gift this is! You are not at the mercy of something outside yourself to accomplish this cleansing process, for you hold in your hands the incredible tool of spiritual WILL, a tool that enables you to accurately perceive, cleanse, correct, and illuminate anything you identify as needing transformation. Walk in the faith that your Team is also continuously assisting you in neutralizing this negativity, for this is an integral part of your mission together.

It is true that energy cannot be destroyed, but it can certainly be redirected. Therefore, the "neutralization" to which I refer is actually a process of vibrational elevation, which removes the dross and points the force in a higher direction, much like the chaff is removed from inedible raw wheat so it may become a source of nourishment. Therefore, it is this powerful will that you are after, not Light, for *you are already comprised of the most exquisite and effusive Light conceivable-I* promise you this. You need only to exercise your will to clear the path for your light to fully manifest.

Imagine a little baby wishing he were made out of the soft, beautiful skin that he sees on his mother's face. Only a baby could possibly think something like this, because only babies are unaware that they are already made of the very same thing as their natural mother! This is the caliber of your thoughts when you wistfully yearn that you could be a Light being like others who you admire, that you wish you could shine this Light into the world-you are thinking the thoughts of a baby. My dears, you are literally *made* of Light, glorious Light! Just open the doors with your will and the Light shall pour forth, just as you aspire for it to do. Open those doors, and keep them open with the exuberant force of joy. The rest will develop automatically.

When you enter the Earth, you embrace a sense of individualism so you may live the life of a human being. On the Other Side, we may recognize one another as individuals, but we experience each other in unity. Our spiritual bodies overlap at different points, creating a beautiful bonding. If you could see this, you would be witness to unique colors that are created by the overlapping energy fields. Glistening golds overlap breathtaking blues at one point, then vibrant greens with effusive silvers at another point, creating colors that I truly cannot describe as similar to anything on the Earth. Any words I choose to use will cause you to conjure up colors in your mind with which you are familiar; I know not how to describe a totally new hue to you. Actually, this lack of adequate word association is a limitation I'm grappling with throughout this entire discourse. In reality, it's your spiritual imagination that I am striving to arouse, not your literal mind.

There is such a whirl of living, pulsating misty beauty in the realm wherein I now reside! It's a kind of ether that actually breathes! And yet the Earth is still a part of the glorious spectacle available to me. Through my new "lens" I can perceive that the Earth plane is amazingly fluid and changing. All the solidness you live with appears as constantly shifting, shimmering masses, waves of overlapping colors and dancing vibrations, all held together by the power of humanity's collective concentration. You are all joined in mental agreement with the physical structures and living species around you, and so you actually participate in their continuing existence with your personal concentrated energy. You create your environment en masse, in a sense, with your common beliefs, for you depend upon the continuation of the plants, animals, mineral, and certain social structures for your earthly education. In fact, all living things participate in upholding the structures and life forms needed there.

This interconnectedness is why people are able to commune with the energy of a tree, animal, or anything else upon the earth. Every human being has a little bit of plant, mineral, and animal within their body, which provides a wonderful mix of vibrations through which the soul can operate, a mix that enables you to relate to and connect with all forms of life. Energy fields are real, and they do not remain in neat little packages. You, your loved ones, animals, plants, water, sunlight, people everywhere and even those you might call your enemies are constantly radiating their essences across each other's energy fields, causing flurries of continuous emotional exchanges among everything organic. This principle is operating according to an impersonal law and results in conditions that you interpret as both edifying and painful. Your emotional nature is the mirror of this field, and through it you can view how enlivening or how draining a particular blending of energies has been on you. You are not as separate as you think yourselves to be, from each other or from the other living things of the earth, and certainly not from your Team. Indeed, if you had the eyes to see, you would be able to watch rolling balls of energy, streams of vibratory intentions, waves of intersecting fields, and oscillating points of sparkling light swirling all about you and others at any given moment. These energies have an impact on you; for this reason, we encourage you to generate the best energies you can possibly offer, knowing that *what you generate is what you will also be shielded and guided with.*

The Earth is filled with these vibratory memories. You have the bones and archeological finds to prove it on a physical level, but there is just as much if not more invisible residual energy of past events lingering in the animals, the rocks, the rivers, the mountains, the forests, the seas, and so forth. These memories act as magnetic markers that draw our souls back to certain continents, places, people and experiences. When we or our Teammates revisit the Earth, we sort of take up where we left off, instinctively knowing where we "left our magnets". As we begin living out our span of days, we fervently seek for them without actually being aware of what is driving us to those particular places, pastimes or people. Some of these magnets have such a powerful influence over us, we cannot help but passionately commit ourselves to their cause, while the pull of others may be so weak, we tarry near them only for a moment. Some haunt us until we complete a certain task, and others we sense so slightly, we almost ignore them. But have no doubt-the draw of these magnets is at work in every life.

Your choice of nations, families, field of work, education, politics, causes, alliances, goals and so forth are not random. They are the product of magnetic forces that you and your Teammates have left behind or placed in advance of your arrival to guide you in your walk through illusion towards your destiny, and are an integral part of your guidance system.

The Earth is a dimension wherein compassion is the saving grace of humanity. *You have entered this particular dimension to develop compassion* and to learn how to consistently express this compassion even in times of great difficulty. While there, you will also stumble and commit errors that need to be forgiven by others, *thereby providing them with the opportunity to exercise compassion.* You are all mirrors for each other, and just as we dislike mirrors that do not present us in the best light, we tend to reject our fellow human "mirrors" when they do so as well.

I share with you the purest commandment: Forgive everyone everything instantly, before contempt takes root in your heart. It is possible to learn to see the mistakes of others not as individualized flaws, but as part of the collective illusion we all embrace when we pass through the Earth filter and by doing so, spare yourself much difficulty. If you do not forgive instantly, you are simply putting off what will have to be done later. In the meantime, you are radiating the energy of non-forgiveness out into the ether where it will quickly find other vibrations of non-forgiveness to bond and multiply with.

If you find yourself in a state of bitterness, then try to pray for the person or situation you cannot forgive, for you cannot hate someone for whom you pray. Perhaps all you can utter is, "I release you/this situation to Universal Law." This is enough to make a strong start, for it will allow you to turn your mind away from preoccupation with the person.

When you are ready, allow the words "There but for the grace of God, go I," to become your touchstone. Are you kind, disciplined, and gentle? You were not always this way. Are you talented, giving, and caring? There was a lifetime that you were the opposite, and a wise one looked past your exterior, recognized the light buried in your heart, and awakened it. Try to remember this when you feel emotions of anger and condemnation towards another rising up within you, and recognize this as "your turn" . . . your turn to be the one who sees the light that is latent in another. Begin with the premise that each person carries within themselves the same divine spark that you do, and *speak to that light!* Only light understands light, so *speak to that light with the language of your light.* Have faith, for your soul is fluent in this language.

What you give to others, you create for yourself. Is there something in your life that needs forgiveness? Do you hope that others might be able to see past your less than honorable words and actions into the essence of your real self and give you the chance to make amends? What is it you ultimately want to reap? Whatever it may be, seize the day and choose to sow it *now* by offering to another that which you need yourself. Pay this gift forward, and watch your life heal in ways you never imagined.

THE CORE

The core of the team is a reflection of the core of the soul, and functions in the same way. The soul is composed of three primary energies, a trinity of forces. These energies blend with one another in the following fashion: imagine two lines intersecting, with a third line draped across and around the other two, like a banner or sash. These lines or forces can be envisioned in this way:

Down-Love
Across-Will
Diagonal-Grace through Spiritual Legacy

These energies whirl circularly clockwise to form a blending of color and vibration that is the spiritual body, the emanation of the soul. Love is the core of the soul. It pulsates continuously as does the heart-rhythmical, constant, swelling and receding. Envision it in your mind as an oval shape of brilliant pink energy, diffusive in texture, warm and inviting, irresistible.

This core is made up of the kind of Love you feel when your child who has been gone so long appears on the horizon, heading home at last. It's the prodigal son kind of Love, the kind of Love that wipes away all judgment, fear and hurt. It's the kind of Love that empowers us to walk through fire to save someone or to forgive the seemingly unforgivable. It's a noble kind of Love, pure and vulnerable, bearing the sort of beauty that stops people in their tracks and drops people to their knees in awe.

This Love is crossed by a lightning bolt of Will, a crackling streak of silver and gold that is continuously oscillating with an intense power. This Will is strengthened in the friction of the Earth, where we use it to assert our creative natures and pierce the darkness so Love may be shined into the shadows. When maintained by conscious direction, it is our protector. Even at its lowest ebb, it nonetheless shields our essence of Love just as the sternum shields the heart, while in its strongest form, it manifests miracles.

Grace is an element created by your spiritual legacy, and appears on the spiritual body as a diagonal banner or sash worn across and around the other two elements, Will and Love. In essence, it holds the other two aspects of the soul together like an honorary belt of badges. It's such an amazing and beautiful concept, one that has the power to "stir up your mind to pure remembrance," once it's fully grasped. This concept of legacy can reveal to you who you and others really are, and what function you are each fulfilling for one another, as well as what placeholder you are filling out in the strand of connections that comprise your Team.

Grace is the saving stamp of our spiritual elders, our Team, and our spiritual parents. It is equivalent to the DNA of the body. Your physical body is sealed with the genes of your biological ancestry, stretching back far into antiquity. Similarly, your soul is branded by the spiritual legacy of your spiritual family. This seal of Grace is your key to your spiritual family's Akashic records. It is the comfort of your Spiritual Mother's embrace and the wrapped-around support of your Spiritual Father. It is the power of your spiritual grandparents and the wisdom of your spiritual great-grandparents and all those beyond them. It is the finishing touch of beauty and elegance upon your soul, your direct line to your lineage, a lineage encompassing pairs of masters. The blending of these various personal lineages ensures that a huge variety of degrees of spiritual DNA will be poured into the Teams, yielding greater access to multiple gifts.

When you better understand the construction of your spiritual body, you better understand your Team, for the latter is modeled after the former. This is your core, your essence – Love, Will, and Grace. Likewise, this is the core structure of your Team, with various members working as primary agents for one of the three primary aspects. Of course there is a natural overlapping of abilities and duties, just as you find in any group, but each is dedicated to upholding one in particular.

I know now that my mission there was to work in the field of Love, which activated the elements of Grace and Will within others. Just as a spark can initiate a series of light bursts, each of us activates other aspects in those we encounter. If you honestly scrutinize your lives, it will not be difficult for you to recognize with which component you are primarily working. Remember, you have a main mission in one of these areas, and while you may at times take over temporarily in another area for someone else, you are more intensely connected to one aspect more than the others.

Share your beauty, my dear ones, in the purest way you can, to as many as you can… while you can.

WHERE I AM

Eternal bands of beauty stretch before me in symphonic and choral layers of harmony that never stop and are ever evolving. I hear only what my ears permit me to hear, but here my "ears" are my consciousness, the one I've strengthened in the "workout gym" for the soul. Although I know that the music echoes eternally, I am content with the portion that is available to me, for I know it is all I can comprehend at this time. I am living within the fullness of the law of my own being, and I am at home within it. It may help you to understand this by thinking about how deeply you appreciate a symphony when it is played for you, even though you cannot play it yourself. You are content and appreciative that such beauty exists, not frustrated that you are not a musician on stage; *indeed, your part as a listener, with a heart bursting with appreciation and bliss, is just as vital as the part played by the performers.* The same principle is active here. I rejoice in both my participation and my receptivity to that which is beyond me.

The segment I hear, though unique to my surroundings, sounds complete to me, for it carries the echoes from the higher realms within it. When a tuning fork is struck, strings around it vibrate and pick up the sound and energy. In the same way, what I am conscious of is a mixture of sounds that are in my immediate vicinity mixed with those not in my vicinity. In this way the symphony has a reverberation of sorts that stirs my soul to its highest potential response.

I am singing, of course. Everyone is. You know how lovely and rare it is on earth when someone passes you on the street humming or singing something beautiful? You wish that everyone could be so "tuned in" to that uninhibited spirit of spontaneity that motivates one to sing out freely. Here, all are in the chorus and the singing is everywhere, with precise and unusual harmonies that occur as we overlap one another in varying degrees. This blending of our spiritual bodies creates exquisite harmonies. Why singing? Because it's pure vibration… only we do it not only with our voices but our entire body-it is the sound we emanate from our essence.

This is happening on the Earth as well. Every individual is radiating a sound, a vibration, that is not usually audible or visible, but most certainly present. And without realizing it, you are all reacting to one another's vibrations. These emanations are what you are sensing when your intuition kicks in about someone, some place, or some activity. This is why it is so important that you learn, through trial and progress (some call this trial and error), to use your interpretive abilities regarding these intuited vibrations, to obey your reactions to certain conditions and individuals. Intuition is one of your greatest protectors — use it wisely! While it's true that when vibrations of love combine, they oscillate at a high level, the opposite is just as true. For this reason, it is imperative that you listen carefully to your intuition.

My awareness of the eternally expanding spheres above me is much like your multi-faceted awareness when you are traveling. You are in New York and see the people and their activities there as contrasted to Florida, where part of your mind remains. You attend a symposium on Africa, and ponder the conditions there, conditions that are vibrantly real to you even though you have never been there.

You think about the mystery of death even as you marvel at the approaching birth of your grandchild, and you think about how in this very instant, millions are dying while millions are being born at the same time. You are aware that it's freezing here, and know it is warm in another place, but you shelve that information for a while, so as to focus with what it is that you are presently experiencing. However, that other information never leaves you. And, though your main focus remains on one or the other topic for a given time, you are nonetheless processing all these things at once. Quite simply, your human awareness is broad enough to hold multiple streams of information in your mind while focusing on a specific choice. Just as you multi-task, you also multi-comprehend. When you are ready to change your focus from any one of these components, you shift your attention and energy in a new direction.

This shift of attention is exactly what occurs in death. The focus of the soul is simply transferred away from the body and towards the dimension that lies before, as if you've decided to walk out of the confines of a small room into a gloriously refreshing garden. Once there, you are immersed in the grand beauty before you, and all your essence flows in that direction. You are fully aware of other directions, but adjust your frequency to your new abode just as you adjust your wardrobe to suit the event you are attending.

The grandest expansion you are capable of imagining may give you a sense of the freedom of which I speak, and yet there is no way for me to put the breadth of clarity and the depth of comprehension that's available on the Other Side into words that you could fully fathom. I suppose "availability" is the best word I can find. Your highest mental capabilities upon the Earth cannot make available to you what is available here, any more than fresh bananas are available at the North Pole! Still, it's vitally important to reach for the vision, *for only in reaching beyond your own unique and very personalized limitations do you ever progress.*

For this reason, it's important for you to honestly assess your weaknesses. Everyone has them. Does it really matter if yours is weakness A, B or C? Why are you so afraid of them when you are so well-equipped to confront them?   Your soul is far more powerful than they are. Can it be that perhaps you've actually become attached to them, identifying with them as a comfortable and familiar part of who you are? Some people actually enjoy the drama they spin around their weaknesses and are hesitant to let them go. *If you are truly determined to do more than give lip service to transforming these weaknesses, we encourage you to regard them as nothing more than weights you've chosen to lift in order to strengthen your spiritual muscles.*

In order to accomplish this, be open to having an up-front chat with yourself and your team about what strengths you have to build upon and what frailties you need to overcome. Remove emotionalism from this process and approach yourself objectively, rationally and kindly, as you would a dear friend. There is no reason for either shame or pride. You are simply admitting that you are like everyone else, a soul enrolled in a school of compassion facing certain tests. Why shuffle along burdened by masks and illusions when you have the opportunity to fly on wings of authenticity?

When you leave a state of Individuation and enter a state of Reemergence on the Other Side, what becomes available to you in the new environment is tremendously increased, much like a goldfish that grows larger when you put it into a bigger tank. This includes your view of your strengths and weaknesses — from this height, they are seen *as the part of the picture that they truly are, not as the exaggerated issues they appear to be on Earth.* All things are seen in their proper perspective. It's as if you are no longer living in a valley, but vie—wing things as from a mountain peak, with the whole vista rolled out before you at once — all the valleys, lakes, oceans, cliffs and meadows.

Not only that, you also have the ability to take it all in simultaneously, as if you suddenly had many eyes rather than two and an expanded brain that can fathom each piece of the picture instantly. Your perception shifts from that of a camera shutter that allows only a fragment of the picture to be viewed to one similar to the scope of a panoramic camera. You are like a child who goes up in a plane and exclaims, "I can see my house, the pier by the beach, the whole city, all at once!" There it all is, in one fell swoop, far more glorious than it ever appeared when you were on the ground, but so familiar at the same time. "Ah, yes, I remember!" you say.

You remember so many things, most profoundly your beloved Teammates and the plans you'd made together. You also recall that *you chose to enter a highly focused course of study on the Earth*, which explains why certain issues loomed large in your experience. You needed them to, just as a student needs a magnifying glass to complete a course in biology. You realize you've been involved in a very specialized project, which required intense scrutiny of some details. Once you leave the Earth environment, the details take their rightful place in the vast scope of your existence.

But it's not all remembering — it's also the awareness of the exploration that still remains, because there is forever a horizon, a horizon which represents your next aspiration, *for growth is eternal* and ever based upon the same essential Universal Principles which recur over and over, on every level of existence. As I speak of this scope of vision, I am stirred to remind you that this dimension I am in is not more desirable, or "better" than the one you are living in. These various environments that our souls enter are just that-environments. Consciousness is the only reality, and is not dependent upon any "location" of the soul. You are exploring the Earth for a limited time, much as a sailor goes forth for a while to see what lies in distant lands. That exploration does not define the totality of who that sailor really is. It is only one of the many temporary experiences in life that he has chosen. The Earth is your current land of exploration, and it's a most wonderful school *designed to teach you how to exert your true essence while operating in a field of distractions and a wide variety of vibrations.*

Therefore, I want so much to instill in you the realization that the Earth is an incredible, rare, and exciting dimension established specifically for the development of spiritual stability, wisdom, compassion, and creativity. *Your planet is a treasure,* a place to be appreciated, protected, and used for your highest good. This is a large part of the purpose behind this message-to *foster within you a powerful awareness of the presence of your Team and to teach you of the marvelous opportunities for advancement that the Earth offers you.* You are blessed to have a body to use as a vehicle for discovery, and are exceedingly blessed to have access to the immense amount of information and wisdom that is so freely shared in the world today. May you be comforted and encouraged by this description of where I am but more importantly, may you be empowered *right where you are* so you may learn to live abundantly in whatever dimension you enter, cognizant that there will be many more to come, for change is the first law of the Universe.

ACCELERATION

When you have a Teammate so deeply dedicated to her mission on Earth and to those she so profoundly loves, she brings to the Other Side a tremendous amount of insight. Not only is her passion for her mission and her personal connection to her Earth companions extremely powerful, but she's also "fresh from the conference" so to speak! She has returned from the meeting astounded, filled with ideas, enthusiasm and energy. She's ready to give her report, and while doing so, she's absolutely bouncing off the walls with excitement, filled with the richness of her recent experiences on Earth, eager to express her concerns and creative ideas of how to improve things. She is reviewing it all with the blinders stripped off, seeing how, "This worked beautifully there. But over there, I could have tried this, or I could have tried that but I couldn't see it at the time."

In this atmosphere of heightened clarity and "vibrational now," the Team has the advantage of sight in all directions — a level of seeing which includes hindsight, foresight and insight — all at once. By consciously and deliberately bonding with your Team, you can more closely link your visual vantage point with theirs. Like the multiple lenses in the eyes of bees, the Team combines its perspective into a full circle, thereby expanding the whole. Your teammates absorb your viewpoint, and you may absorb theirs, in degree. *This blending of viewpoints and its resultant expansion of perception is the key to accelerating your spiritual growth.*

All efforts towards accelerated spiritual growth are celebrated with great joy by the Team! If only you could hear the cheers, see the excitement, taste the uncorked champagne when a member chooses to accelerate through deliberately sped-up efforts. A group of wildly cheering parents at a ball game can't begin to compare with the peak of jubilation seen here. That isn't to say that minor achievements are not recognized. Any achievement you make, no matter how small, filters into the Team, and the gain is shared and instantly felt throughout the ranks. But when a member consciously ratchets it up, the joy is ineffable!

You may examine earthly parallels to understand how acceleration occurs. Look at how an athlete builds muscle, a musician masters a difficult passage, or a student graduates college early. The answer is no mystery… it is by increasing study time, picking up the pace, and setting new standards for oneself. Many times, it is simply *applying what you already know* to what's right before your eyes. Ask yourself, "Am I truly using everything available within myself and around me to better my life and those I encounter?"

Consider how industrious-minded pioneers made do with every scrap of food and supplies they could find to create a new life in a new land. The same scenario occurs with spiritual matters. When the soul is passionately committed to completing her quest, outer conditions cannot prevent her success. There are those who have access to volumes of inspirational material, superior education, and every kind of physical comfort, yet declare they cannot find time to pray, meditate, or reach out to someone in need. On the other hand, there are those who have not one of these opportunities and comforts, but manage to structure their entire lives around spiritual practices. Clearly, what makes a person reach for the depths of wisdom is not the ease with which things flow in their lives. This fact is so clear to me now from where I am, I must say to you: *Excuses only delay the fulfillment of your destiny; determination to press onward, irrespective of conditions, accelerates it.*

Without a doubt, applying what you learn is essential to your progress, but let us not underestimate the power of thought alone. Deliberate visualization is a powerful tool, both in practical and spiritual matters. Athletes and musicians in particular employ the method of consciously induced experiences through imagination, for what you call daydreaming is actually an integral part of the creative process. If you cannot imagine something, how can you create it?

It's a fact that visualizing oneself hitting the ball or playing the piano keys turns on parts of the brain that affect performance just as surely as actual practice does. So it is with spiritual acceleration techniques — the use of your spiritual imagination is a great enhancer. The Biblical words, "Whatsoever things are true, honest, just, pure, lovely, and of good report; if there be any virtue and if there be any praise, *think then on these things*," are divine advice, for your thoughts feed your mind as directly as food feeds your body. The more beauty, forgiveness, kindness, and peace you visualize on a regular basis, the more you will discover these things in the people you meet and the places you go.

Take ten minutes a day to see in your mind's eye the good things you wish to manifest, and you will have helped to make them so. Take more time, and your contribution will be greater. Visualize freedom and happiness for your friends, family, *and those people who are difficult in your life*, acting and speaking from a place of gentleness and love, and you can rest assured they will be affected by your vision of them. Most importantly, you will begin to look at them with more compassionate eyes. They will appear different to you, and the difference in your belief will be felt by them at a subtle level, causing a chain reaction.

Last but not least, v*isualize others accelerating in their spiritual growth* and look for ways to quietly support and serve them. You cannot help another soul learn without learning more yourself. The greatest gift you can give another is to cherish their essence and rejoice in their growth more than you do your own. When you are with someone, they are the most important person for you to encounter at that time, or you wouldn't encounter them. Regard them with eyes of encouragement and kindness, for you never know who they truly are.

When considering the concept of accelerated development, remember that your goal will not be reached through a straining, rigid, or forced manner. Those feelings may initially arise as we begin to clumsily seek what we're after, but a grim, heavy-hearted approach to something that is not truly akin to one's nature is never the answer to our prayer. In fact, it is completely pointless to drive ourselves towards anything that is not natural for us, just as it is pointless for a first grader to attempt lifting (much less reading) a huge, cumbersome college textbook. Imagine how painful it would be to watch such a little one struggle to carry a book twice her size and watch her grieve because she could not yet read it. In the same way, the Team does not want this fruitless and uncomfortable experience for you. Instead, you are encouraged to keep your step light and your heart open and grateful, content to learn gradually and naturally with joy and sincerity, knowing that if you do so, opportunities to take the "additional classes" that are appropriate for you will surely come your way.

The truth is, the moment of absolute dedication to the unfolding of one's divine nature happens without our full awareness most of the time, for it develops unattached to the analyzing worries of the mind or the struggling emotions of the body, in a deep inner chamber of the soul. This is most aptly compared to how a caterpillar can only be transmuted into a butterfly while it is in the cocoon. It emerges *not dressed up in a new outer veil, but in a totally reformed state*. Its transformation is authentic and complete, one that could never be contrived, forced, or pretended. Have no doubt, the Team is primed to recognize those momentous turning points of true illumination, and all the heavens back them in their response to it. This is how it happens. . .

"THE CRY"

When the yearning of the soul to rise up like a blazing torch in the night becomes an utterly overpowering urge, one's heart sends forth a call, a cry as it were, which is heard by one's Team. This sound, like a beloved's familiar voice, or the cry of a child for its mother, is so recognizable, so poignantly stimulating to the Team, that a response is then activated within the core of each one of the members. Without the authenticity of this cry, such a response cannot occur, for the Team is operating in accord with Universal Law, and their ears are uniquely attuned to recognize this cry. This is not merely a cry for help, a cry of demand, or the curious mind's cry for more experience. Rather, it is the cry of the soul's essence, filled with humility, understanding, appreciation, devotion and profound sincerity. It is the cry that no mother can deny, that all of Nature and the angels rally to answer, for it is the cry of one who is not only ready for the breakthrough of spiritual acceleration, but who has without any hesitation emptied him/herself for that singular purpose.

Indeed, it is this emptying that creates the cry, for only in the echo of that valley of emptiness can the cry resound. It is a literal sound, an actual vibration, which cannot be imitated or created by conscious conviction, for it only occurs deep within the secret, fervent chambers of one's individual identity. This vibration pulses across the Universe, like a stimulating signal, a code in a sense, and in accordance with Universal Law, the response from the Team *must* come. Instantly and with great passion, they galvanize themselves to activate in full force the banner of grace that crisscrosses the spiritual body! Points along the banner begin to glow as never before, filling the other two aspects, Love and Will, with all the collective legacy of wisdom of the Ancient Ones, the spiritual family's DNA, and the genetic links that are components of the soul's makeup but have been latent until now. Through this legacy nourishment is passed, sustaining and uplifting the individual as never before. *Memories are activated, divine connections are intensified, and streams of information begin to flow.* It is as if a floodgate has been opened that leads to a world of other channels, and the inundation begins, pouring in from numerous sources and directions.

The seeker will never be the same. He will abandon many things very quickly that simply have no use or value to him anymore. He will find himself emboldened by the clear and obvious change this has wrought, and many things will fall away or be added, as naturally as breathing. Doubts and limitations will cease, for they will be ignored as their smallness becomes overpoweringly evident, like someone who has suddenly noticed that their dwelling is far too small to live in any longer. *This seeker will now, without question, step into the shoes that have been waiting for him for eons.* It will be the most natural thing for him to embrace the lifestyle of a spiritually accelerated student, characterized by the following:

Honoring – The seeker honors the Light of God, her portion of divinity, and all members of the Team, consciously and unceasingly, with a continuous proclamation of unity that sings through her soul.

Obeying – The seeker obeys the voice of intuition and direction, recognized as a combination of the Team's instruction and his own inner guidance. Nothing brings him greater joy and security than to obey this beloved voice.

Asking – The seeker's first prayer upon arising and last upon sleeping is to receive, reveal, and revere authentic truth in its rawest form, and to be protected from illusionary thoughts that are encumbered by ego. Her every breath is an asking that she be purified at the core level of intention so that nothing can sully the integrity of information, intuition, support, insight, and resources that the Team is offering. She wants nothing to distract her from the most authentic and valid spiritual work for which she might be used.

Observing – The seeker watches and listens as an objective observer to the messages within Nature that flow to him each day — what the moon, sun, stars, wind, rain, plants, and animals have to teach him. He knows that the Earth is a reflection of Universal Law, passed through a materialization filter, and that it is here to teach us volumes about that law. He "seeks not to be understood, but to understand."

Prioritizing – The seeker makes the process of communion her priority, secondary to all else she does. She infuses all other aspects of her life with this priority, not the other way around.

Thanking – Grace is the greatest gift, the gift that supplies the bridge across which we all must pass in our evolution. No soul crosses the bridge without help. The seeker is unspeakably grateful for this bridge, and in this keenly aware state, she is incapable of dishonoring it. Her dedication to the mission of the Team has become unshakable.

These are the primary characteristics of the change that has been wrought in the seeker's soul, and it is permanent, for this is not the phase of back and forth experimentation, questioning and exploring, but the stepping over into a frontier from which there is never any return. Nothing could bring the seeker greater joy than being released from the instability of those earlier courses to the surety of this land that lies before him, bursting with unrivaled beauty. Without a backward glance, he steps forward and begins to walk home, led by the unseen hands of the Team.

THE CHOICE TO INDIVIDUATE

Entering human form is a choice, not a mandate, and what compels us to return to this form once again is inexorably entwined with our natural desire to assist the Earth's evolution by learning, teaching, building, and rebuilding. During a life review, we become keenly aware of what contributions we have made to the upliftment and healing of lives upon the Earth. This review occurs in relation to the attainable possibilities for that point of consciousness in the way that tests are created for a certain subject matter for the grade that is being tested. In other words, the ideals selected by that soul for that life are appropriate for that individual, relative to nothing or anything else but the soul's own capacities and scope of vision. Just as the question for a two year old is not, "Have you learned to drive?" but "Have you learned to walk?" so does the soul know well the vision it had for its lifetime, and this is the standard by which it conducts the review with the Team.

We all know the feeling of deep contentment that we experience when we see a worthy goal come to fruition in our lives. We also know the feeling of disappointment in ourselves when we do not see it come to fruition. And again, we know the difference between lack of fruition that is the result of our own poor choices and lack of fruition that is the result of others' poor choices. Perhaps we led a friend to drink from the waters of happiness, and they chose to turn away. How different this is from simply being too apathetic to lead our friend there in the first place.

From this standpoint is a life reviewed. Guidance is offered but never forced; judgment and condemnation do not exist. From this point of clarity, *where possibilities are contrasted with actual accomplishments*, does the soul decide its next course of action. At times, one may consider re-entering the Earth immediately as its best option, so eager is his desire to correct something or complete something while it is still fresh in his experience. Or, this quick return may be chosen because he wants to be with the same family members to correct or finish a task or to bolster a dear loved one who he can see will soon need him. In such a case, the soul is regarding this quick re-entry as essentially a continuation of the same lifetime, not a totally new one.

Some souls may need to remain on the Other Side to heal and fortify themselves before entering Earth again. At other times, souls may choose to wait until certain Teammates have completed their phase of work before they return to begin the next phase. Or, the soul may choose an entirely different school of learning in the future, for many other dimensions and galaxies provide unique of learning opportunities quite different from the Earth. As you can see, there is a great deal of variety in the decisions made by teams.

The choice a soul makes concerning a particular life's conditions may be easier for you to understand if you compare it to situations you may have experienced already on the Earth. Imagine a scenario where you have had a disagreement with another person, and as you analyze the incident, you make a decision as to how to respond. There are a number of alternative ways of responding, and you hope you are choosing the wisest one. Perhaps you feel such a powerful yearning to set things right with your friend that you pursue her relentlessly, seeking ways to correct the pain inflicted or to understand the pain directed at you. You may feel that you can't rest until you make peace with that person, or at least exhaust every available means trying.

This is the same impulse that draws one back to the Earth – the determination within oneself to infuse a greater degree of Light into a particular situation. It is the natural impulse of the soul to do so, and it is always a choice; however, it is a choice that one would never shirk, any more than you would turn away from the cry of your own child. So great is the beauty of what you are able to witness on the Other Side, if you see any gap between a lesser choice that you made while upon the Earth and the higher alternative that was available to you at that time, you are compelled to find a way to close that gap, whatever it takes.

The tools used in closing that gap are the same ones that propel us in all our strivings — the three main components of our nature: Will, Love, and Grace — nothing more and nothing less. These powerful impulses drive us all on every level to fulfill what we know in our deepest parts to be true. You may rest assured that the conclusions you arrive at during your life review will be the best decision possible and as a result, will be regarded by all involved as a positive step.

Therefore, drop all ideas of punishment or fear in regard to this subject; in fact, it is best to think less about reincarnation or karma and more about the fact that *there is really only one continuous lifetime* lived through many bodies and on many planes. And there are many options available other than life upon the Earth. *From the Other Side, the idea of separate lifetimes evaporates as the continuity of the soul's existence becomes clear.* It all appears more like phases of existence, not separate lives that begin and end. These phases appear to flow smoothly one into the other, no more separate than how a day, a night, and the next day appear to you.

This brings us to the consideration of methods to consciously address "loose ends" while still in the physical body. The requirement for this very powerful system of completing your soul commitments is to use the kind of honesty that the soul uses after death in assessing its recent life. *Yes, it is possible to conduct part of your life review while still in the physical body.* Here are some points to guide you:

First, consider your physical conditions:

1. Scan your body with the eyes of the soul. Look at every square inch of it. Your body is an incredible reflection of Universal Law. Therefore, it is truly a temple for your soul, constructed out of the same "stuff" of the spiritual body, but in a far denser form. Examine each hair, down to each toe. Acknowledge with gratefulness this tool for your use, and ask yourself, "Do I use the body's abilities to enhance my growth and the growth of others, or do I waste its usefulness on activities or inactivities that produce either neutrality or harm? Is my state of health due to personal negligence or an outside problem? Either way, what can I do to honor my body with adequate care to ensure and preserve its functioning?"

2. "What is my current earthly situation in regard to financial security and work conditions?" The answer to this question is not merely how much money you make or where you live or work, but relates to the vibratory degree of positive energy you are generating through your work and/or your money. Trace your attitudes towards finances back to your earliest childhood memories to see the pattern you have created in this area of life. Notice the changes you have made along the way as you learned more about these topics. Honestly assess what needs to be done to bring this part of your life into harmony today. Again, the goal is not to think in terms of greater financial gain but *greater harmony with your true destiny.*

3. Consider the relationships in your life that are the closest, and ask yourself the following questions. Then do the same with more distant relationships. Remember, only absolute honesty will allow you to glean any progress. Also remember that it is not necessary to discuss this with

the people you are considering. This is an inner exercise, and the things you realize will manifest without words in your future interactions with them.

a. What is my gut-level reaction when I think of this person, and what is my secondary reaction? What is the cause of this reaction? What have I done to contribute to the reaction I am having to this person?

b. When I recall incidences of joy and disharmony with this person, in what ways did each of us offer through vibration the energy that we exchanged? What segment of the exchange am I responsible for?

c. Do I regularly radiate vibrations of wellbeing and happiness towards this person? Or do I experience twinges of jealousy, revenge, and condemnation towards him/her? Do I assign the guilt of error to him, without recognizing my hand in it? Do I have secret hopes that this person will fail or experience pain? Do I feel a smug satisfaction when this person struggles, believing this to be what she has coming? (Please note that it's important to see the difference between sympathetically seeing the weaknesses of a person and cynically judging him when we see those weaknesses manifesting.) If anyone fits this category in your life, make him/her the object of your daily priority prayers. Emanate peace and hope to him, envelop him in your best wishes, mentally take a humble position beside him, and he will sense this in you from afar. At the time of your next meeting, things will begin to change.

d. "Who or what am I neglecting?" This question usually brings about an immediate response within a person. We all have opportunities to uplift others that we are neglecting to respond to, for upliftment takes effort, takes emptying, takes humility to achieve. Our minds throw out all kinds of reasons why we don't have time to nurture this person or that person, but if we simply take the first step, life's pressures will begin to prioritize themselves. Including this person in our meditations is also an authentic way to launch the impulse within ourselves and activate the other person's receptivity to our outreach.

4. "What perceived blessings and hardships am I living with?" It may startle you to learn that what appear to be blessings and hardships are *exactly equal in their purpose*: to give us opportunities to grow. Consider this: what appears to be a blessing, such as a life of ease, is actually demanding of us *the very same thing* that a life of struggle is demanding: to be a beacon of Light in the midst of the illusion we are walking through. Are we resting upon our laurels because we have the blessings of beauty, talent or material objects, so it's easy to coast along on those things? Similarly, are we resting upon our laurels because we've given up in discouragement over our difficult life? If both are yielding the same result — in this case, apathy — then what is the difference, really? *Both are providing an opportunity to learn the very same lesson*, for both are posing the same question — what shall we do within this situation to infuse more compassion and love into our lives and the lives of others?

Take the time to scrutinize these things in your life, and suspend judgment as to whether or not they are categorized as "blessings" or "hardships". From the spiritual vista, they are neither. They are only vibratory conditions that we either use to support or undermine our spiritual progress. Make a list of these things in your life, and with total frankness, assess them, every excuse set aside.

These are only some of the kinds of questions that the soul seeking Truth can ask along the journey. There are many more, each of which comes to us when we are ready. It is a choice — ask these questions now or ask them at a future date. Either way, they must be faced squarely, not because we are forced to do so, but because *the soul desires this knowledge*, this uncovered, unpretentious reality, as much as the body desires its next breath of air. Truth is the soul's oxygen; therefore, embrace Truth bravely; only advancement can follow! Fear not the process of unveiling the mirror. The liberation that you will ultimately experience is far beyond any degree of joy you have ever known.

Remember, your Team is showering you at all times with unconditional love. Nothing that you reveal to yourself is invisible to them, and *their vision of you is always in your purest form*. They uphold this image of you at all times, seeing you as a beautiful ray of light they sent forth to carry a message to humanity. Every soul has its message to carry, embedded in its spiritual DNA. Your weaknesses, in the eyes of your Teammates, are nothing more than mud caked upon the face and hands of a darling child after he has snuck outside and played in the dirt. The mother knows once the thickness of the mud is assessed, the water drawn from the well, the fire lit to warm the water, the tub prepared, the soap added, the washcloth employed, and the rinse completed, that same sweet countenance will again be visible, and even more precious than before. Associate this image of a loving, forgiving mother bathing her little one with the kind of support offered by your Team, and press onward without fear or shame. Step up to the nobility of your true legacy, now.

BODY AND SOUL

The senses of the body are an exquisite tool for the use of the soul. Bodies in all stages of health and in all conditions have immeasurable usefulness. A body that is impaired is treated by the soul as water treats blockages in a stream through which it flows — it simply finds a way to circumvent the situation. As water always finds its way around a limitation, usually in a very innovative fashion, so does the soul know how to make the best use of whatever form it joins.

The soul uses specific aspects of the body more intensely at certain times, much like certain parts of a car's engine are more revved up during certain stages of driving. Likewise, a soul may intensify a function of the body for its purposes, enlivening a certain part of the brain or physique to accomplish a certain feat. Consider how often profound or beautiful works of art come through what appear to be "regular" or even "mediocre" people. This is because a certain part of their nature has been hugely fortified by the soul, so it appears to be unusually advanced. You can observe this phenomenon when a nondescript kind of person suddenly transforms into a grand speaker or a socially maladapted person performs a noble act. In such cases, the soul has greatly magnified the talent for a specific purpose.

At times, the soul wearies of the body, of curbing and molding it, and removes its influence from it, much like a child who tires of caring for a pet. In other words, the soul, while remaining tethered to the body, withdraws its attention, and the body continues on automatic pilot. The child returns to find his pet sick or depressed and then must get to work to correct the situation. So does a soul of weak willpower create for itself through neglect or procrastination a dilemma that it must correct, not because it is being "punished" but because it is simply experiencing the causes and effects of the creative process. Hopefully, a child learns how to be responsible with a pet before becoming a parent just as he learns how to shape things with play-dough before going on to use real sculptor's clay. So does the soul grow in strength by exerting its influence more and more consistently upon the wild impulses of the emotions and the body.   Never forget, the union of your unique soul and your current body is a miraculous occurrence, *an opportunity that was designed with great care by a Team that loves you and is profoundly invested in you.* It is a combination of the spiritual and physical that *will never again be repeated in the same exact form,* and is therefore worthy of your deepest appreciation and most sincere efforts.

PARALLEL VIBRATIONS

You may choose in your current lifetime to correct an issue that has troubled you by employing the law of parallel vibrations. Before delving into this, please understand the use of the word "law" in these teachings.

Universal Law is the beloved friend of the soul, the net into which the soul falls when unsure, and the hope on which the soul stands. Here, I have no fear of these laws any more than you have fear of the law of gravity, which makes your life on Earth possible. However, we certainly respect these laws, for we know their influence on us is unyielding. You build your lives upon the ever-present security of this law of gravity, and utilize it as your greatest friend, do you not? You rely upon it to supply you with the framework you need to do everything from constructing houses to growing food, and even when you defy it, as when you go up in an airplane, you rely on it for your safe return.

So is the law of parallel vibrations to the soul. Conditions in your life can change for the better when you act positively upon one circumstance in your life that involves principles that are similar to another circumstance that appears out of your control. In other words, it is not always necessary to address the person or the place in which you feel you fell short. You can transform what occurred in that place and that time by focusing your heightened awareness upon a new, yet similar place and time — *a parallel set of situational vibrations.*

For example, if you delayed your own education through laziness, you can literally wipe that slate clean by supporting another person's education. If you, like the prodigal son, have squandered your gifts and regret your choices, you may redeem them by recognizing and fostering them in another. *Whatever it is that you wish you could change in your perceived past, you may cleanse through actions in the present.* We use here the words "your past, present and future" *yet we actually mean your perceived past, perceived present, and perceived future.* Remember, linear time only exists while you are in form. Out of form, where things are unfiltered, there is a simultaneous quality to events. So instead of the sense of moving back and forth along a horizontal line, there is a sense of moving up and down in a vertical line. *Therefore, your present actions actually move back to regenerate the past, and this renewed past moves forward to affect your present.*

To help you understand this, imagine a person committing an act of violence. Then, sometime in the future, after considerable regret and retrospection, that person dedicates his life to counseling victims of violence. The energy generated in the person's act of recompense travels back (instantaneously) to raise the vibration of violence created in the (perceived) past. This newly healed vibration moves forward in time and returns to the same person, causing a new door to wisdom to open for him. If he enters that door, an even higher vibration is generated, and it in turn goes back to the past to raise the vibration of the original violent event to an even higher level. This renewed vibration moves forward in time and returns to the same person which creates yet another door for him to enter... and so the cycle continues, back and forth through what you call time and space, or up and down in what we call the "eternal now" until the violent vibration has been completely transformed, healed and purified. Each of these healed and heightened strands of vibration creates another possible reality which is available not only to the individual who committed the violent act but to *everyone who was affected directly or indirectly by that act.* Each soul involved is vibrationally elevated as each new door of opportunity is entered. In this manner, all things are made whole.

Once this beautiful process becomes real to you, you'll find that opportunities to heal any hurts in your perceived past start to suddenly appear more and more frequently. A chance to help a child may come along that requires you to do what you did not do for some other child. A chance to care for an elderly person may present itself, allowing you to give to him what you were unable to give before to another. A chance to protect an animal may come, allowing you to compensate for the neglect of a previous animal. A chance to act with loyalty and integrity at work may come, allowing you to heal a former negative work situation.

Whatever form these chances take, strive to recognize them for what they are, and gratefully grasp the opportunity they offer to reconfigure the events of your perceived past. When the student is ready, the teacher will come, so be ready, willing, and alert for what may arrive on your doorstep. *Remember, they are parallels, not coincidences,* sent for the purpose of healing and recompense, not only for you but for all who are affected by the situation in question, *whether in the past, present or future.*

BANDS AND POINTS OF CONSCIOUSNESS

We often talk about levels of consciousness, but perhaps a better phrase would be "points of consciousness." Take the image of a Christmas tree. You have brilliant lights, dimmer lights, large ornaments and small ornaments. Truly, if you had a tree with nothing but gigantic ornaments and lights, you wouldn't have the beauty created by the delicate points of light enmeshed in between the larger ones.

It's important to understand that the little lights are actually enormous lights, as grand as any other, but they are hidden behind a thick wall of illusion so that only a peep hole is available for the light to come through. Gradually, this wall is dissolved, until the light becomes more and more visible. During this period of gradual dissolving, we have the appearance of a small light. Nonetheless, this little point of light is a glorious treasure, just like a baby. Do we respect an infant less because she cannot speak yet? No, we marvel at her potential instead.

When the essential value of every point of light is truly understood, any pride associated with spiritual evolution vanishes. It is pointless to consider oneself as superior to any other, for growth is eternal. Therefore, there is always a bigger light, a more purified vessel, a wider horizon — eternally, eternally! There is no ceiling to this evolution, because everything you're doing pushes those above you upward, and everything done by the levels beneath you push *you* even higher. So we are all standing on each other's shoulders in a sense. You would fall without those levels beneath you to stand upon. You need those shoulders beneath you, and they need you above, inspiring them onward. It's such a beautiful harmony of evolution.

Words cannot describe the beauty created by the lovely baby lights that provide a beautiful backdrop to everything else. They are radiant dots of hopeful, eager aspirations, *and they include all our own points of consciousness, even our former selves, still shining!* You have this phenomena happening throughout physical space at all times. The stars you are seeing now may have burned out long ago (in other words, transformed into another state of existence) and yet their vibration, their degree of light, is still visible to you as you gaze up into the sky, and may be for millions of years to come.

So it is with our former states of being, our own baby dots of light, *our own selves that we still see,* yet no longer identify with. Those baby lights remain as *symbols of our former selves*, connecting us to those who are presently at that stage of growth. This is why one quality of spiritual maturity is the ability to feel compassion for and understand the nature of other points of consciousness. The Master knows he/she has walked in those shoes.

When we look at old photos, we experience this automatically, reliving our state of mind at the time a certain photo was taken. We recall the situation we were living in at the time, how we felt, what job we had, where we lived, and how our lives were going in general. We absorb all this in a flash as we gaze at the photo, even though we are not in that state of mind anymore. Still, the photo remains to remind us of what we went through to get to the point we are now.

Respecting our former selves for the stepping-stones they provided to us is the first step to respecting all the other bands and points of consciousness around us.

Therefore, strive to feel compassion for your own former weaker self, for this will help you overcome the tendency to categorize any other point of consciousness as beneath you. You will always have endless bands of consciousness above you and endless bands beneath *and to the side of you.* If you didn't have these bands around you, feeding their energy up and down to you, *reinforcing your lessons by providing you with a parade of contrasting possibilities to watch*, there would be instead a kind of emptiness, and everyone from the top down would slide. There is a literal "trickle down" and "trickle up" effect to growth.

Indeed, we are resting upon each other, and all those baby dots, those lights on the tree or within those bands — whatever image helps you the most — are all vitally important. They are upholding the evolution of everything. If you own an office building, how long will that company last if no one is the janitor? How long will the CEO in his top floor office be able to work without the electrician and window washer? How would one learn a skill if they never made a mistake that could show them which possibility of action to avoid? We learn as much from observing the errors of others as we do from making our own errors — this is a stark reality. You cannot possibly function without the bands beneath and around you holding up that segment. It's a system, a real system.

These bands are like building blocks. Some souls move quickly through the bands, others more slowly, some start over, some repeat part of it and don't repeat another part. Some are incredibly advanced in certain areas, and incredibly weak in other areas, so they're rather lopsided, sort of like a person with one leg shorter than the other, but it all blends together to create the One. No matter where you think you are, or what you think you're doing, just try your utmost to *fill out your layer.* That is all that is asked of you. Of course, if you want to double it up, you can. If you want to triple it, you can. If you want to make it ten times faster and more powerful, you can. Whatever you do, do it from a place of great enthusiasm, joy, love, and authentic humility, *respecting the efforts of those around you.* Foremostly, let your thoughts and actions be filled with authentic gratitude for those upon whom you lean and stand as well as gratitude for those who are far, far beyond you, pulling you up with their energy. Everyone is pushing up and pulling up, so we're all moving together. At times, positions are even exchanged. How can we not appreciate each and every soul? It is this gratefulness, coupled with your absolute love of learning and sharing truth, which will automatically accelerate your growth.

Remember, though, sometimes you choose to accelerate and sometimes you don't! In some phases of life you will, and in some you won't. At times you will "stay put" to enrich the level you are upon rather than moving on quickly. Resist the tendency to label the value everything and everyone. Most certainly, don't condemn another for how much or how little he applies his truth. No life can be compared to another, for each life and each Team is unique. Don't put a *lazy* label on this person, or a *holy* label on that person. Maybe one is just having their "second cup of coffee" in this lifetime, while the other has made commitments of a different kind. You may be bustling with spiritual activity, and they are still asleep. Do you feel critical of people in another time zone who are sleeping while you are awake? Of course not! In fact, you wait until it is the right hour in their time zone to even call them. Extend this spiritual courtesy to others. Indeed, extend it to yourself.

When you recognize what you need to do *for your own growth*, run with it. It's the most effective way to get others to run anyway — just start running. You know how some people will jokingly stand and point up at the sky to see how many people will gather around them and look up at their imaginary vision? Inevitably, a crowd quickly gathers. As they look upward, people see a variety of things that they think the other person must have been pointing at! In other words, they see what they are ready to see. Let this playful image be your guide, *as you lead by example*. You'll know if you're on track. You'll know by the results, the way you feel, the effect you have on other people, and by the people who enter and leave your sphere of influence. Be happy, be happy! There is so much support and enthusiasm available to you from your Teammates. That's why

I always said, "Don't take things so seriously" because this stuff should be truly inebriating, in the highest sense of that word. Remember that everything you encounter represents a point of light in a band of consciousness, including yourself, and walk on in faith.

SPIRITUAL INVIGORATORS

One might think of a spiritual master or great teacher as a type of spiritual "invigorator." These Team leaders work within every single band, even what appears to be the most depraved states, and they certainly don't always manifest as saints in that mix. God reaches out to meet everyone wherever they are, and some Team members agree to work in extremely dark vibratory situations so they can be a presence in the midst of those struggling lives. Therefore, we have no concept of who is really whom, where they really are, or what they are really doing.

The generalization of "master" is far overused, for there are eternal stages of attainment. No one reaches "the top," and no one attains some final victory. Rather, there are many points of completion along the way, a wide variety of missions accomplished and celebrated, which yield the next vision of a mission. In addition, we may "attain" in some areas while remaining incomplete in other areas, just as in your Earth lives you have areas of great strength and other areas that remain undeveloped.

If these invigorators were not present at every level, the banner of grace could not function as it does. Just like DNA in the physical body has switches that turn on at certain points of a fetus's development, so does a soul have spiritual DNA that requires stimulation before it can manifest. For example, a child who appears to be quite ordinary might have a tremendous gift, but if someone doesn't come along to expose him to conditions that develop that gift, to stimulate the glimmer, to activate and launch that DNA within him, it might not get woken up at that particular time. So the master's presence at every level is a quickening agent designed to wake up, activate, and launch the spiritual DNA in other souls, wherever they may be. Your Teammates have the backup of all these resources available to them, and are eager to make it available to you by providing you with encounters with higher mentors. These mentors may connect with you in physical form or from the Other Side.

Bear in mind that these mentors may not always come in the form that you think they would or should. No truer words have been spoken than "every person is my teacher". From my perspective now, my comprehension of everyone's role in my life is immeasurably expanded. I feel nothing but profound gratefulness to everyone for who they are and the experiences they brought into my vibratory field there. In many cases, people are not at all who I thought they were. It's a delightful surprise when the masks come off! Therefore, consciously strive to use every interaction with another person as an opportunity to observe, learn, teach, and connect with *the true identity* of that person rather than the mask they have fashioned for themselves. *Learn to regard other people with the amazement you typically save for rare and precious things — for this what they truly are!*

As you observe someone, *feel* the miraculous fact that they have a Team of their own, that they are on a great and glorious adventure, just as you are, that they have had a wide variety of experiences that you perhaps cannot fathom, and that they possess their own special view of the world. Who knows who they really are? Indeed, they may be a spiritual invigorator. They may be your next mentor. At the least, there is always something you can learn from them.

By approaching others with this mindset, you will attract teachable moments to yourself on every turn. Have faith in your Team, who are always working to send the best teachers and instructive situations your way. Remain open to those who come to teach you. "Ask, and it shall be given. Knock and it shall be opened."

THE HODGEPODGE THAT IS THE EARTH

Consciousness is the only reality and now is the only time. I want to say that again, for it is so accurate. *Consciousness is the only reality and now is the only time!*

This is to say that:
1) Nothing is real to you unless you are conscious of it, and 2) All you need for growth is compressed into the present moment, the eternal now.

Everything you're looking at in the physical world was, at some arrested point in time, someone's perception of consciousness, whether we are talking about a thimble or a grand architectural structure. Consider a sculpture that stands frozen in Time in a museum. That sculpture is a symbol of a particular moment of awareness in someone's consciousness, and everyone continues to collectively uphold that symbol once they've experienced it, for they attach a part of themselves to it. Once we've acknowledged something, there it is forever in a sense, even though the consciousness that originally produced it will grow and evolve into something else. Just as we have physical memories, our various perceptions become our spiritual memories. In other words, whatever is created by a point of consciousness remains, either in form or idea, as a marker of that time/space event.

It's sort of like a child that makes some funny little drawing and gives it to you with great glee. A few months later, the child might be drawing something much more elaborate, but *he has left behind the symbol of where his abilities lay at that earlier point in time.* In fact, you can hold the symbol of that child's skill and sweetness in your two hands. Consciousness and matter have merged in that simple drawing, quite an incredible thing. *The reason it seems so commonplace is because absolutely all of creation is doing the same thing, all the time.* It is the one great and universal process.

Someday you and the child, now a young adult, may look at the drawing and say, "I remember the day..." You laugh about it, or perhaps cry about it, depending on what memory from the past you are sharing. You recognize that it is a symbol of a different time and that was considered the "now" at that time. It is a point of consciousness that is still interesting to you, but not relevant or even real anymore, for in the "new now" that child may have evolved into someone who is capable of producing advanced works of art. Only the symbol of how her mind once worked remains as a kind of marker along the way.

Expand this concept out to include absolutely every concrete item upon the Earth, and you can see why there exists such a tremendous hodgepodge of manifestations. They are simply endless collections of symbols, types of landmarks and placeholders that represent where everybody has been at every point in history.

You have all around you amazing works of architecture, art and music, and then right around the corner you have war museums and streaks of hate graffiti. These contrasts are everywhere, each one of them created by someone's thoughts at some point along the way. They are memories in tangible form, containing vibrations that have the power to spark the traveling of one's consciousness to that particular juxtaposition of time and space.

To some people, these objects are mere curiosities. For others, they are extremely relevant feelings-in-form that impact every aspect of their lives. The neighborhood park you pass each day may have little value to you, while to someone else, it represents a lifetime of meaningful moments. In this way you can see that consciousness — whether individual or collective — is what infuses everything with meaning.

This is why you may see an exquisite carving right next to a sign that bears a slogan of prejudice. Both are manifestations of a point of consciousness frozen in time at a certain location. Although there is a huge gap in the quality of each of these objects, *the less refined symbol is actually the more refined symbol "in becoming," for all vibrations are engaged in the process of evolving.* It is entirely possible that the carver was the one who wrote the hateful slogan at an earlier time in his life, or even in a previous lifetime. He may have been filled with rage at that time, rage which he gradually learned to heal and redirect, moving on to become a sensitive, gentle person who expressed those attributes in his beautiful carvings.

From my perspective now, I can see how many times contrasting symbols are created by the same person in different stages of their lives or in different phases of history. What is it you are most passionate about helping to change in the world? *Most likely, in another time you were involved in creating a lower quality symbol and have returned, determined to upgrade your contribution to the Earth.* Therefore, though it may be hard to accept, the truth is you may be carrying placards for equality today because you once signed your name on the dotted line to wage war.

No matter how these symbols are created, they are always representative of where someone's thinking was at some time, and despite the fact that those who created them progressed beyond them, they remain with us, repelling or attracting their viewers. Just as the Earth is still filled with the artifacts of civilizations gone by that tell us the story of that era, so do such objects and structures serve to represent human evolution and devolution, every increment of the way.

As you look at these things, you may sometimes feel revulsion and ask, "Why must there be that expanse of concrete instead of a field of flowers? Why was a beautiful forest destroyed to build this building?" We are not saying that you will love all the symbols that you see, only that it is wise to look at them through the eyes of the soul. Strive to gaze upon these symbols in all their forms without judging, simply acknowledging how they came to be, realizing that you are simply looking at what various points of consciousness, *including your own*, have created throughout the centuries.

Can you imagine the breathtaking beauty that lay before the settlers when they came to your land? They stood upon the mountains and looked out over a virgin country that had never been damaged by the indigenous peoples. There were endless acres of lush forests and fields filled with streams and rivers of living waters. In such an unsullied state, Nature is a perfect parallel to the higher realms; this is what was gifted to humanity.

Look what was done to it all. Look what remains. You cannot in all fairness say, "Look what *they* did to it" because you were very likely a part of that story. So simply say, "Look what we have done. These sites of destruction, this pollution, these cruelties, are the symbols, the markers which all humanity, *of which I am a part,* have left upon the Earth."

Indeed, you may lament the ignorance or greed that caused the damage, but you cannot categorically blame others. The revulsion you feel within yourself when you see the harm that has been done to the Earth and many of its inhabitants is due to the fact that *you are recognizing your own handiwork in that destruction*. Your feelings of revulsion are there to guide you, to push you to create beautiful, refined symbols upon the Earth henceforth.

Next, with objectivity and compassion ask yourself: Were those settlers really capable of creating something different? Were the majority of them aware of concepts of ecological preservation? Did they have the foresight you have today about environmental impact?

Indeed, there were some who blew the trumpet of alarm, but they were greatly outnumbered. Few of them had the intellectual, educational, economical, and scientific resources to do anything different, and even if they'd had the development, they didn't have the tools to implement and maintain that vision. So their human ingenuity was directed into the creation of that which was of immediate necessity, resulting in the relentless assault upon the land and its indigenous people.

You can be certain, though, that there were those among them who made higher choices, though you may not have heard of them. Oftentimes spiritual invigorators work behind the scenes or are not recognized during their lifetime. But without doubt, their offerings resulted in many of the measures that were eventually enacted towards preserving and protecting natural resources. Team members are always seeking the opportunity to intervene and uplift where it is possible, even when their interventions are completely invisible to the generation receiving their help.

What would occur if this land lay before you today, if somehow humans discovered a new continent on the Earth that had never been seen before, another expanse of unpolluted, undamaged land? Indeed, there are those that would rush in to do the very same thing — tear it to pieces as they erected symbols of their point of consciousness. But there are many, *many*, people on the Earth today who would enter that land with the purest of intentions and say, "What if we preserve it, what if we protect it, what if we develop it around the finest of ecological principles, or even better, what if we do nothing at all and allow it to rest in pristine purity?"

Yes, there are enough people today with the capacity to hold up that vision, act upon it, and most of all, *maintain it.* How remarkable it is that all the seeds for that enlightened viewpoint were planted long, long ago when some points of consciousness provided the negative contrast needed for higher points to respond with passion towards the better choice. All this is to say that none of us is in any position to condemn another nation or generation of people. Rather, we are to seek out ways to use the tools we have to uplift conditions for humanity, fully aware that the area we are called to serve in is precisely the area we once did damage. We are all in the process of creating new, higher symbols alongside our old ones. *We are all painting over our own graffiti.*

Armed with this viewpoint on the symbolic impact of material objects, coupled with an understanding of your own contribution to negative conditions that exist upon the Earth *as well your capacity to become part of the solution*, it is hoped that you may now commit yourself to casting your attention upon the most beautiful symbols that you can possibly find, and offering your best energy to creating many more of them. In this way, you will help bring the more exquisite symbols to the forefront of human existence and thereby participate more powerfully in the mission of divine manifestation that is unfolding upon the Earth today. Ask your Team to assist you in discovering the best that the Earth has to offer so you may duplicate that beauty in every aspect of your life. Seek to view, experience, and uphold works of value for their loveliness, efficiency, usefulness, power to uplift, and power to heal. Then create more of them yourself, *for once you have seen this principle in action, you are responsible for applying it to your life.*

HUMAN INGENUITY

There is a tendency among people who are seeking spiritual knowledge to regard the Earth as a place of pain, a dark dimension filled with threats. There is no denying that your body and its brain, which has as its primary focus survival, acquisition, defense of assets, reproduction and protection of offspring, spends much of its time in following these instincts. These are the instincts that keep the structure of the planet intact, and are not to be dismissed. But beyond these instincts is an amazing force, *quite unique to the Earth experience*, a force I am calling "human ingenuity". This force is produced by the energy created when a soul and a body combine together, a blending that results in a rare opportunity for creative experimentation. Access to this force is one of the main reasons a soul chooses the Earth as its school.

When one makes the decision to blend oneself with a body, it is done out of the sparkling joy for the chance to create with concrete items. The Earth is a magical place, really, where ideas can be sculpted into physical form. It's the place where a director can gaze at a blank stage, knowing he has the freedom to produce a show right out of his own imagination. It's the place where a dance choreographer gets to take the movements she sees in her mind, consider the abilities of her dancers, and blend this information together to create the most beautiful dance possible. It's the place where a business owner can come up with a wonderful product, market it, and improve lives. It's the place where an architect may visualize and then design a fantastic structure. It's the place where a painter can experience the thrill of that first brush stroke as she attempts to transfer thought to visual form. It is the place where a healer can regenerate tissue. Yes, this is the joy of entering the Earth, the thrill of pitting oneself against what limitations are there to see what you can make of it — the place where we get to explore and play with human ingenuity.

When an athlete decides how to hit the ball, hundreds of impressions go through his head-the distance of the ball, the strength of his body, the wind, the angle, his position on the court or field, and so much more. All this is calculated in a split second before he decides how to react. This kind of evaluation about what limitations exist and what materials are available to create with is the challenge and the pleasure of living on the Earth. It can be felt in the smallest of things, such as deciding to rearrange the furniture in a room just for the fun of it, to the largest of things, such as the restructuring of a nation's government. It is the reason we put our feet on the ground each day — to see what we can make out of the sculpting clay that is our lives.

I don't need to tell you that many people from time to time, and sometimes permanently, lose the zest for this creative process. It's rare that it can be sustained without some degree of ebb and flow. Focusing on human ingenuity can help you retain your enthusiasm for life! Reminding yourself regularly of why you came to Earth in the first place — why everybody has come — is worth the time and effort. Stop throughout the day, close your eyes for just a moment, and feel it in your body, your mind, your hands, and your heart. Appreciate it! *It is an honor to partake of it, and to be there using it at this time in history.*

Be willing to drop the idea that physical life as something to be endured and tolerated until it is over. You have an absolute smorgasbord of choices spread out before you, yet so often you take the variety offered for granted. *Make use of what is there for you learn, teach, celebrate, and overcome.* You have not come to simply drift through life on placid waters. You have come to pit yourself against the tides, to "catch some waves," *to practice using your spiritual muscles.* So don't be afraid, resentful, or cynical when things come along that push you to do just that. Look at those challenges as opportunities to prove to yourself what you are really made of.

Appreciating the smorgasbord of life doesn't mean you have to spend all your valuable energy scattering yourself across the landscape in an attempt to try it all. It would be exhausting to do so, and there is so much there to choose from, you would become ill if you tasted it all. There are also many things on that smorgasbord table that are not in harmony with your particular point of consciousness. Whatever you do choose to participate in, give it your all as you join in the game of creating through ingenuity. *There is always something you can do to make even the tiniest moment a little bit better.* Don't delude yourself into thinking you have to wait for the big moments or you will waste precious opportunities. A smile, a kind word, a helping hand… *these small gestures open doors that lead to the "big things".*

The wise teachers who come into the Earth to lead and inspire others also use this wondrous tool of ingenuity. They arrive with all their spiritual tools sharpened to see what they can create. They know they will encounter an element of resistance, and they have taken this into consideration. The storms of life do not deter them, for they understand the cause and purpose of these storms. They also know they have the power of the Team behind them, and a connection with a Light that cannot fail to uplift once it is activated. They fully recognize, respect, appreciate, cultivate, develop and utilize this connection. They work with constant conscious awareness of the process and laws at work, both physically and spiritually, and direct them with purposeful skill and *unconditional love* which they've perfected through practice. They join the physical realm not because they personally need the experience, but because they love their Teammates so dearly and yearn so greatly to assist the many souls who are walking the pathway of spiritual development, they want to offer their support. Filled with compassion, they enter the great river of physical life with a boat they've built with their own hands so they may cast life rafts of hope to all they meet…

These writings are one of those life rafts, cast by our Team to those who have magnetically called for it. Remember, the waters may be choppy at times, but your raft is tethered to a boat so large, nothing can disturb it. Hold fast to the hands of your Teammates, who are also holding onto the hands of higher Teams... and have no fear.

FAITH IN FRUITION

So much of what we send forth in the form of hopes for ourselves or for others, we receive no validation of. We yearn for our loved ones to make certain strides, and we pray so intensely to grow. Where does all that aspiration go?

I can tell you without hesitation, it hits the mark. That's where it goes. I beseech you to maintain faith in this fact, for it's more than just a comforting notion. When? Where? The answer is here. The Other Side is not called "heaven" for nothing! It is the place *where the highest potentialities of any and all efforts that were initiated from a place of purity in our souls come to fruition.*

In your present state, you have the illusion of delays caused by Time and the receptivity of the object of your focus. Please know that from the Other Side, your arrow has hit its mark, according to its degree of motive and intensity. Whether or not you can see it concretely happening in the Earth, rest assured it is unfolding. There is always so much more going on than we are aware of. Let this fact bring you confidence, boldness, bravery. Bear in mind that whether you can sense it or not, you are not acting alone! You may be an individual, but you are also a conduit for your Team. The visions, intuitions, creations, and impulses you are having while joined with a physical body are not only from you. They are extensions of sorts, an echo as it were, of the Team behind you.

As we saw in the analogy of a speaker presenting information at a conference, a company representative may *appear* to be a single entity, but he certainly isn't relative to the information flowing through him. He is a mouthpiece, a mirror, a channel, a vessel, a symbol of an entire company. He is well aware that the outcome of the conference is essentially unknown, but the possible gains are so important, he is ready to take on the expense of the conference and the challenge of the work. He knows he will be sharing ideas with a group who may or may not be ready to accept what he has to offer. The seeds he plants at that convention may not blossom right away, or even in his lifetime. The only thing he knows for sure is that he has set a ball rolling, which will make some kind of an impact somewhere, somehow, down the line.

In the same way, you are offering who you are to the world, and we are offering who we are to you. There are Teams above us who are offering their insights to us as well, and Teams above them who are doing the same. The stream of guidance is eternal and infinite. There is no guarantee that our efforts will be well received, for no outcome is written in stone — but this is not our concern. Our part is to simply offer. And the same is true of you.

Oh, there is such power in ideation! When you tap into a higher order and write a glorious song, you have sent forth something that has tremendous influence on the Earth, *even if it is never heard by anyone.* This is because it is the flowering of a pure and loving seed within you. If the song happens to be produced, the singers and musicians are infused with its vibration concretely. If it is publicly performed, a larger group experiences it, processes it through their particular set of interpretative abilities, and absorbs it according to their degree of receptivity. However, it is the process of writing it where the greatest work is done, because the writing process is the initial up-reach and thereby captures the version closest to the source. Once the song is released from its source, it is subject to the quality of the voice, instruments, sound equipment and the ears and brains of those who will interpret it.

Your loving spiritual impulses work in exactly the same manner. Yes, you want them to lead to concrete manifestations, but their greatest power is in that point of pure origination. Therefore, work primarily on your purity of motives, recognizing that this is your greatest tool for manifesting the resources and creative energy that are of use to humanity.

Have faith that in the heavenly dimension, those motives are received and "made so" in their most pristine state. Here, the hopes we have for our children thrive and come to fruition. Here, all songs sound as they were first intended. Here, all artistic expression exists without the limitations of materials. Here, all Nature blossoms without the stain of neglect. And here, all things imaginable that originated in the soul's deep chambers of highest intention exist without the dilution of the Earth filter. This is what faith means — to continue to radiate the purest of intentions you can muster, no matter how they are received upon the Earth, certain that the Team honors them and keeps them for you in safekeeping upon your return. Have Faith!

ACTIVATING THE ALTERNATIVE

Within every family or community there are individuals who are more closely aligned with one another than with others. A natural affinity or friction exists between some members, and it is there for a very productive reason. This deliberate mixing of points of consciousness and degrees of affinity is for the purpose of promoting growth among all members.

It is true that souls with close ties and similarities come together to provide a "safe port" for one another, camaraderie, and friendship. They may cluster in a group for bursts of concentrated study that they then take out into their personal environments. But even within harmonious groups, there is great diversity. *A mixture of energies is needed on Earth to supply the kind of contrast in conditions that stimulate the soul's surge towards the highest plane it can reach.* Necessity is the Mother of Invention, and we choose the light only when we see darkness for what it truly is. Combining contrasting types of people ensure a more heterogeneous evolution. This diversity is present not only in families but in communities, organizations, and entire nations. Taken to its widest application, it's an explanation for the condition of the entire planet.

This is why we encourage you to avoid at all costs categorizing people's state of consciousness by your own checklist of standards. The most difficult, lost soul could be making more progress *in relation to his overall point of consciousness* than the spiritually advanced one who has dropped the ball when it comes to his part of his Team's mission. Remember the words in Hebrews: "Be not forgetful to entertain strangers: for thereby some have entertained angels unawares."

Concerning the concept of respect for the spiritual path of others, we share the following exercise: If someone directs a negative word, action, or energy at you, do not regard it as such. Instead, choose to validate the potential of that person by visualizing for them what they did not do for themselves. *In other words, imagine for them an alternative behavior.* See them choosing words that are kind and actions that are wise, even as they do the opposite. In this manner you will help them redirect the negative energy they have released.

In your mind, see them taking the high road, fulfilling responsibilities, speaking gently, and so forth, in spite of appearances to the contrary. When you "activate the alternative" for them, you put into motion another chain of events that could have been. The energy behind these ideated events, when directed at the person you are concerned about, *will* eventually have an effect upon their chosen course of behavior, for *thoughts are things.*

The Team is continuously doing this for you, for they are intensely aware of the power of their unified vision to affect the choices people make upon the Earth. You may turn left, but they see you turning right and all the wonders that await you if you go in that direction. In other words, *they hold high the vision of your true capabilities, much as a teacher holds onto the vision of where she wants her students to someday be,* not allowing the day-to-day struggles of learning to diminish her hope of their ultimate achievement.

The vision the teacher carries for the child is so grand, she has no way to describe it to him. How could the child possibly fathom what great literature awaits him when he is just learning to read? Instead, the teacher works with the child at whatever level he is on, encouraging him to fill out that level so he can move on the next. The teacher also knows that to take her student from the primer to the classics, she must not only offer him material on his current level, but must also challenge and inspire him to keep reaching for the stars. To accomplish this, she provides a shelf full of enticingly beautiful books that the child cannot yet read next to those he can, and in this way achieves a *healthy balance between contentment with the present and a hunger for what is to come.*

The same process is in place for spiritual growth, and you can utilize it in your daily life. Not only can you activate alternatives in others, you can activate them within yourself by envisioning yourself in various situations acting, speaking, thinking, and interacting in the manner that you believe is best. Instead of "rehearsing" a speech in your mind that is defensive, accusative, or angry, rehearse one that is forgiving, honest, and wise. Tap into the sage that lies within yourself to prepare for how you will react in the face of any discord that may arise in your life. "Arm yourself" with words that are designed to heal rather than to inflame. Then, in the rush of moments of emotional stress, you will have this planned response to fall back on.

You can apply this method to any situation you are going into where you know there might be tension. *Send out a vision of harmony, acceptance, and goodwill ahead of yourself in order to activate the possibilities that exist.* Become a conscious creator of open doors to positive potential. Bring that vision out of the chambers of the soul into the fray of the day! It can do you no good buried in the realms of wishfulness. You are there to "make it so"!

OSMOSIS

You know from scientific study that osmosis is a process of transferring molecules through a membrane from one side of something to another. In the human body, this is how water moves in and out of cells, a life-sustaining process. Water moves directly through a cell's membrane because the molecules are small enough to do so. Larger molecules cannot enter the membrane, so the cell is protected from things that are not supposed to enter it.

You can use this concept of osmosis to understand the method by which you are uplifted by the Team above you. The "molecules" they offer are more refined, and thus they can pour into you. What you send back to them in the form of vibration is not as refined (due to the Earth's filter), so it's absorbed through a different process that involves the additional step of acceptance, much like you must deliberately go to the mailbox to receive your mail. Your offerings of love and light are regarded by your Team as great treasures.

The exchange of energies through spiritual osmosis is the primary tool for birthing in the heart the desire for change. While no one can do for you what you must do for yourself, osmosis stimulates the aspects of your spiritual body, causing you to lift your eyes to a more beautiful belief, which inspires your higher nature. We all need visions of greater possibilities in order to lift our eyes; otherwise, we simply gaze across our current plateau or let our eyes drift downward. This "looking upward" is what always occurs when you reach out to your spiritual Team.

Your task is to keep your part of the channel open to the Team, beginning and ending each day with receptivity and gratitude, and taking time for small moments of prayer and radiation of goodwill throughout the day. Dedicate each day to the work of the Team. By planning and protecting the time you need for meditation and reflection, you will enter naturally into a free-flowing exchange with the Team rather than a sporadic one, and everything in your life will become filled with ease. *This ease is not because all things will be easy*, or because you will always feel unchallenged and peaceful, but because you will be walking upon a pathway that is illuminated, where "what is *really* going on" is visible to you. It's only logical that when a light is shining on your path and you can see what is really there, you are less likely to stumble.

Becoming a vessel for this discerning Light allows you to view events, individuals, and material things through a set of alternating binoculars (for the expanded view) and microscopes (for the up-close view), whereby the *story behind the story* is evident. Be ready to witness, generate, and undergo tremendous changes as osmosis works its magic in your life. With such a shift in perspective, how could anything remain the same? Be prepared to receive an influx of creative energies that lead to novel spiritual ideas, and know that your Team is behind you as you develop these ideas. Also, remember that even when a new concept is not received at first by the world, your Team is thrilled at the surge of power your fresh ideation has released, for the raw energy behind anything new is so youthful, vibrant, so filled with faith.

You see this in the business world. When a unique idea doesn't go over right away, the inventors adjust it, get feedback, and keep adjusting it based upon what they learn from *both their elders and their peers*. This tweaking is the fundamental process governing the mechanism of ingenuity. So take those ideas and impulses, those unique approaches, those urges to discover bold, new ways of bringing the light into the darkness, and go with it! You will always have tremendous assistance from your Team, and whatever the final outcome of your upsurge may be, you will have generated a strong, fresh impetus that will forever resound throughout the Universe, eventually finding its port of expression.

All points of consciousness are functioning under the same general system of osmosis, yet at different degrees. Think of a school that has kindergarten up to twelfth grade. Every room has similar things in it: tables, chairs, a teacher, equipment, films, books, art material, music, decorations, and so forth. What sets the classes apart is the content that's imparted to the students. A pencil can be used for the simplest task, such as tracing shapes, as well as advanced tasks such as the writing of complicated mathematical problems. The tools are the same; the minds are not. Back and forth the information flows, the teacher sending forth the more refined "molecules" and the students responding with their less refined ones.

The complexity of the subject matter has been built upon the studies of former years, so the algebra student has no right to deride the kindergartener for his current assignment. How much better it would be if, out of respect for his own younger years and those who helped him, he would sit with the child help him write his numbers or count on his fingers. These tasks are in keeping with the great saying, "Service is the price you pay for the space you occupy."

Consider, too, how there are always students within a group who are struggling in one area but wizards in others. So it is within your own nature… you have areas where you excel and areas where you are barely able to keep up with the rest of the class. Still, you are a member of that "grade" so to speak. The whole point of a team is to allow each member to share their gifts to create a fully functioning whole. You do not have to be all things at all times. *Be at peace with completing your portion of the process.* Give what you have to give, and let others shine in their own way. In this manner will you learn to love yourself and others as the Team loves you.

REALIZATIONS

Much is said about the power of thought, but evidence abounds as to how seldom people actually pattern their lives around this power. Life without awareness of one's own thought power is like living without the warmth and light provided by electricity. This power is directly connected to one's point of consciousness, which is stimulated and expanded by a steady stream of realizations.

First, remember that everything you think you know is due to your ability to be conscious, or aware of a given subject. If you sit an infant in front of a painting, she will see either nothing of interest or, at the most, a vague swirl of colors. Even if this painting is of something that will eventually hold delight or great meaning to her — for instance, a playful puppy — you will get no response from her while she is an infant. If her wandering eyes happen to land upon the painting, she will have no reaction to it, no comprehension of what it represents, so in essence she is not actually "seeing" it at all. She is neither indifferent nor stupid. She is simply not yet conscious of the subject matter contained in the painting. She has nothing yet to which she can relate it, nothing to connect it to, nothing to bridge the gap between that image and her current reality.

It is the same with spiritual matters. The Earth is filled with souls who, while experiencing similar things, actually have vastly different ideas about those experiences. Two individuals can look upon the same scene and see the opposite thing from each other. For example, there are those are authentically aware of the song of the trees and the presence of fairies amidst the flowers. On the other hand, there are those who see these same trees as mere interference and want only to cut them down. They are seeing the very same tree, so what is the difference? Nothing but their degree of consciousness, or awareness, about the value of the tree. Now, if the tree-cutter were to have a mystical experience with the trees that opened his eyes to a new reality, he would experience a *realization,* and everything could change for him in a flash. Same person, same tree, new consciousness.

I want you to understand that you are living your life based upon your ability to *partially* see what is within you and around you, *not upon everything that is really there.* Like the infant sitting before the painting, you are aware of your surroundings only in part. In most cases you are extremely aware in some areas and rather unaware in other areas. And it is only through *realizations* that you increase your capacity of such awareness.

Your consciousness is expanded by a multitude of illuminative events, including realizations (spontaneous insights), revelations (received teachings), and clarifications (in-depth information added to something you already know in part). These events are what determine your perception of life, and therefore *they literally create what you call reality.*

Realizations create transformational turning points in your entire stream of existence, for in the moment of realization, everything in your vibratory field changes; therefore, everything in your future changes. And, although it sounds impossible to you in your current dimension, *everything in your past changes as well,* for every new realization connects the dots and fills in more of the puzzle pieces as they relate to the past, causing everything in your past to be *interpreted differently* by you.

Just as you cannot stop interpreting as written words those things that in your childhood were once nothing but curves, lines and squiggles, you will never be able to see things the same again once a realization is experienced. Once the infant comes to see the puppy in the painting, she will never again see the vague swirls on the canvas. She may recall a time when she didn't know what they represented, but *she cannot reverse the understanding of what a puppy is that her mind has now attained.*

Often the Team has information to impart to you which they cannot share until you have experienced certain realizations. They know that their information will have no meaning or value whatsoever until you can connect those dots, build that bridge, and so forth. So they pass along whatever you are ready for, and wait to impart more at the appropriate time. Of course, there is no impatience or judgment in this process, for they know that they, too, are working under the same laws and processes, receiving from higher sources only what they are ready for, according to their consciousness, which is their reality as well.

Realizations along the way, such as those you are learning now, are what the soul feeds upon as it develops, and are the handiwork of the spiritual body: Love, pulsating with absolute devotion, stimulates your Will to pierce the darkness, which activates the power of your own legacy and its resultant Grace. The Team responds to this up-reach and extends itself into your sphere, magnetically drawing you closer as they pour out all you are capable of integrating.

This is what's behind the burst of energy and excitement you feel upon receiving new revelations — that spiritual adrenaline, that joy, that clarity, that surge of hope. Just as the brain's synapses sparkle when intellectual connections are made, so do the synapses of your soul exult when a revelation appears. This, combined with the sensation of your Team's support, causes you to *link your new realization with a corresponding one*, a most important step in the expansion of consciousness. No concept can be put to use if it is isolated from others. It is the integration of the pieces that makes the puzzle whole.

You see this linking of concepts in educational settings all the time. For example, once a student masters multiplication, division can be easily presented to him, but if he has only addition and subtraction under his belt, that leap to division cannot be successfully made. Only after multiplication is understood can the teacher swoop in to say, "You have this concept now — see how it fits with this other one?" In the same way, the realizations you attain are recognized by your Team, at which time they quickly supply links to help you connect to another realization for which you are now primed. Your consciousness shifts slightly, and the entire Team rises higher, as One. Never forget, all personal advances are shared by your Teammates! The information you and they gain are reciprocal.

The feelings that come with clarity are delightful, but the greatest value in that moment is the power of a realization to *change both the future and the past.* Many people have the idea that if they have a stain in their past, it is simply there forever, and all they can do is to live with it and strive to do better. This is a commonplace and logical assumption, but it is only logical on the Earth. Once you are no longer in a physical form, you see that *realizations have the power to reach back in time and reconfigure an event.* You understand that by changing the result of something, the vibration within the events that occurred to cause that result are retroactively changed as well.

As explained before, time, space, future and past do not exist except in your dimension — and they exist there in order that you may more clearly observe principles in action. In a timeless state, *a spiritual change which is authentically wrought becomes the dominant vibration in relation to any given situation, and affects the entire "chain of events"* (which is no longer a chain but condensed into the now).

One analogy for this can be found in your computer. When you choose a new font, you have the power to instantly highlight and change the font of all the words you have typed in the past that relate to that specific document. Your present selection of a new font has transformed all of the old font in an instant. Or, imagine a frozen stream of ice. If you heat the mouth of the stream with an intense enough instrument, the ice will begin to melt all the way back, changing the ice into free-flowing water, transforming the rigidly conditioned past through the power of a new condition in the present.

The image of a stone dropping into water causing ripples to go out in every direction (i.e., your experience of past, present, future) is another way to view this. *Everything is affected simultaneously when that stone drops*, from every angle, not in just one direction. There is no way to know which is the past, present, or future, for the *effect occurs equally on all sides of the dropped stone*.

Keep asking the questions that lead you to new realizations, for this process of connecting the dots and "making real" your insights is your tool of liberation. Remember, the mission is one and the same, whether conducted from the Earth or another dimension. Therefore, your Team is always sending you their highest and most divine emanations and, whether you realize it or not, we are depending on you for the success of our work as well.

RECIPROCAL INFLUENCES

We have spoken a great deal about opening your mind, eyes, and heart to become receptive to your Team's input. But I want you to know that you are also bringing something very beautiful to the process. You are not only calling out for upliftment, not only reaching out with yearning, not only seeking to become more useful and enlightened — you are also making an offering! We are not only assisting you. *You are also assisting us.* We are all partners in this plan, working from different locations but with one vision. Our influence upon one another is reciprocal.

I hope that you understand by now that to the degree you are open to your Team are you a representative of the whole. Fulfillment of the plans we've made as a group occurs when we all open ourselves to one another, permitting each of us to channel each Teammate's gifts. How much more glorious is the music of many strings than that of one single string!

Your receptivity to us is so important, so vital to our Team's work. Can a teacher thrive in a room filled with blank faces and closed minds, her words echoing against a wall of indifference? Contrast that image with a classroom where students are listening, reflecting, sharing, expanding, experimenting, and assembling information, and producing their own version of the concepts, in other words, *creating anew*! This is what you are doing when you listen and react with openness, share with enthusiasm, and attempt to apply what you are learning. Your insight adds to our insight, your excitement adds to ours, your experimentation adds to our body of understanding, for *your growth helps us grow*!

Not only does your growth affect us, your conscious and deliberate efforts at sending us love and support is felt and recognized. This valuable outreach to us occurs in many stages. The first stage can be compared to the kind of offering made by a very young child to an adult. Consider how you feel when a child extends her little hand to give you a flower. It matters not that its petals are crumpled up from the tight grip she had as she raced to share it with you. It matters not that it is as tiny as a clover. It matters not that it is already wilting from the heat, and will retain its beauty only a very short while. It is still an incredible gift, a work of art containing the whole Universe in each tiny petal and the translucent veins that show through its leaves. Most of all, it is still a gesture of love, the kind of love that is overflowing, joyous and real.

When you receive this flower and see the sincerity in the child's eyes, you are transported to the child's place of purity, are you not? You are suddenly linked up to a great goodness that you cannot help but respond to, and carried away upon the winds of hope, a hope that only a child's honesty can yield.

Your humblest offerings are regarded by us in the same way. When you commune with us in any form, (and these forms are endless: music, writing, dance, meditation, prayer, laughter, contemplation, appreciation, and so much more…) then you are giving as well as receiving. When errors are made (and they must be made if there is to be any progress), we all learn. There is no condemnation of an error. Please understand this is a two-way creation, a two-way mission, a two-way flow, which links up with other teams to form a zillion-way creation, mission, and flow. And so, this first stage is precious to us. Oh, how dearly these tender moments of sincere offerings are regarded; we gather them up with such immense affection! They are so important, for they have the unique ability to provide the first uplift, the first penetration of the veil.

The second stage occurs when you absorb enough of the energy of a certain message to have a "eureka" moment. These moments may seem to appear out of the blue, but you've actually been collecting spiritual insights about a certain concept for some time, gradually gleaning tidbits of information and finding pieces to the bigger puzzle, until like in a game show, the phrase suddenly makes sense. That electrifying sensation that comes over you when the puzzle pieces suddenly form an understandable pattern is the result of the burst of vibrations that are released when you become wholly matched to a concept, all edges fitting together perfectly. When this occurs, you may find that you respond with physical sensations such as chills, laughter or even tears, because *what the soul undergoes always impacts the body, leaving the physical evidence of a spiritual event.*

When this state of unity and clarity is felt, you then transfer the joy and power of growth you are experiencing onto your Team through the channel of love that connects us. The wisdom is yours, and yet it becomes everyone's, for it automatically radiates outward and upward to all who can receive it. There is never a resistance or block from our side to the light you have to offer, whether that light is a pinpoint or an explosion.

You may wonder why your insights are so helpful to us, since we already have access to so much from our point of perspective. The answer is simple: all your "eureka" moments are received by us as moments of completion and pleasure, those moments where we become filled with the deepest contentment and the greatest peace, for your achievements are experienced by us as a parent watching their beloved children come into fruition with their talent or character, or a dear friend reaching heights he has striven so long to attain. For us, the feeling that you've grasped an attribute of Truth to the best of your ability is akin to the feeling of fulfillment you might have upon hearing a composition you've composed finally played by a real orchestra. In other words, it makes everything we do worth all the effort.

You can see the parallels to this clearly throughout the world. Accomplishments achieved through teamwork, whether within the family, workplace or community, are one of the greatest pleasure of Earth life. Goals set and fulfilled, hopes vocalized and then made manifest — this is the stuff of dreams. For this reason, we are willing to reach out with every ounce of our beings to offer this information at this specific time in your life, for we know it is the culmination, the fruition, of the efforts of so many souls on so many levels. Truly, nothing is more meaningful to us than seeing this body of Truth grasped and appreciated by you and by all with whom you can share it.

It matters not if the gains made are small or large. What matters is that they are authentic and enduring. We can see the same step taken by various teammates over and over and over, and yet never tire of the pure pleasure of watching that process. Imagine a great maestro who has heard every note of a certain piece of music a thousand times, and yet who still weeps with joy when the symphony he is directing delivers an especially poignant performance. In the same way, your realizations are our symphonies, the fulfillment of our "hours of rehearsal".

In addition, you are experiencing things in our place. In other words, we are able to absorb what you learn just as you absorb what we have learned. You may be "taking a life course" on behalf of all of us, so that we may learn from you without having to take that course directly. *Think about the amazing implications of this for yourself and your Teammates!*

The next stage of your offering is that of overflow, where the ecstasy of a new understanding bursts your personal boundaries and begins to impact others. This overflow can manifest in a variety of forms. It may be that you are given the chance to converse with others about your insights, or that you share reading materials with them, or the fact that something about your aura changes so that you emanate a different level of vibration to others. Then again, it might be that you make major changes in your lifestyle. Whatever form it takes, it represents the branching out of Truth, the flowering of a bud. In this, we celebrate greatly, for this is the ultimate purpose for which we work… to initiate cycles of exploration, extension, expansion, and development.

We need all of you for this purpose. You are the ones who link and leverage our efforts, turning our few fishes and loaves of bread and into thousands for the masses! Each one of you has a portion to carry in this mission, a portion that is designated to be finished upon the Earth. Bear in mind that while our non-earthly state gives us a certain advantage of perception, it does not mean that your boots-on-the-ground position is not valuable to those of us who are in the lookout tower. On the contrary, what you can see, feel, and do there in a concrete manner is the hands-in-the-clay side of our work, and the importance of it cannot be stressed enough.

Is the scout in the valley less important than those that scan the vista through binoculars from the mountaintop? In such a scenario, both are providing the other with timely and relevant information that is crucial to their mutual success. What will make or break their mission is one thing only — *whether or not they can communicate with one another!* Without communication, missions cannot be completed. The mere fact that some of us are working from a different dimension does not alter the reality that our mission is one and the same. Remember, when you transition out of your body, you will continue your mission, and some of us who are in the lookout tower will take our turn in the trenches. Those who continue upon the Earth will remain as dear to you and as important an ally as they are now.

The next, most delightful stage of your outreach to us, is that of witnessing you taking a truth and "making it your own," for this is the stage where you unleash your own powers of creativity and apply what you have learned in a manner that is uniquely stamped with your own brand. It is equivalent to seeing someone not only read what another has written, but write her own material, not only trace a shape on paper, but create an image wholly from his own mind, not only appreciate a garden, but design her own. Just as complete synthesis is the goal in any kind of schooling, so it is with spiritual matters. When you understand the basic principles at work in the Universe, you begin to play with them, to experiment, to dabble, and it's when this dabbling turns into concrete creations that the Team as a whole can be said to have "fully arrived" in relation to that particular concept. *This allows us all to move onward and upward*, expanding into the next great adventure.

The channels among Teams are not the only channels at work here. There is also a horizontal network that is constantly in use. In other words, just as you are affecting us and we are affecting you, others are interchanging wisdom and knowledge with you, side by side. Right now upon the Earth, there are legions of scientists experimenting with the principles of the Universe to see what incredible things they can invent. Likewise, there are millions of musicians toying with the finite set of notes that the human ear is able to hear in order to create an infinite variety of compositions. At the same time, there are scores of architects devising incredible blueprints for structures that will amaze the world in the future. Of course, you cannot consciously see and hear all of these things at once, but *nonetheless the thoughts and creations of these people are affecting you*.

Ripples of cleverness, artistry, and creativity are flowing forth from every corner of the world towards each of you and from you to each of them. Therefore, the ideas and impulses that you wake up with each day are, in part, influenced by the work of all other minds. You are all simultaneously influencing one another with your work, whether or not you ever meet. Like children building sandcastles side by side on the playground, immersed in their own little world, so are all thinkers, inventors, composers, creators, dreamers, builders, and craftsmen of the Earth participating in similar "parallel play". Side by side you build, using the same principles, the same creative urge, the same willpower to forge ahead, yet so often unaware of how your energy is affecting one another.

I urge you to allow the enormity of this process to impress itself upon your mind, for it is a wonderful and integral part of your existence. If all this is going on upon the Earth, think how much more is going on in the higher dimensions, where thoughts and their resultant manifestations are instantaneous! Embrace this process as it whirls around and through you, sending forth acknowledgement, respect and gratitude to the companions who are contributing so much to your evolution, both on the Earth and on the Other Side.

And so, in the spirit of this message, I pour out to you our appreciation for your offerings, large and small, for your commitment to this precious mission, and for your trust in all of us. I thank you for your willingness to hold me and all the Team in a place of love and reverence in your mind, for Divine Love is an energy that always heals and protects, and can cross all illusions of time, space, or distance. Your love for me is a comforting and dependable cloud upon which I can rest in peace, confident that a welcome mat for connection is always there. As you offer this to us, never forget that what is being extended to you in return is just as certain, just as whole, just as reverent, and vastly moreso, for it is totally unencumbered by any resistance or friction.

Accept this enlivening, healing and enriching flow, and bask in that contentment, allowing the steady exchange between all of you there and all of us here to become one of an effortless, confident knowing. Remember! We are an open door to you; be ye evermore also the same.

SPIRITUAL WILL

When we refer to spiritual will, we are referring not to the kind of will you assert *against* anything. Rather, it is the kind of will you assert *for* something. There is a great deal of confusion among people about this subject; it is very easy for people to get turned around. The tendency is to think the purpose of will is to suppress and discipline, when actually it's there to bolster the other aspects of your spiritual body, Grace and Love. Rather than using your will to knock things over, you want to use your will to build things up. In the Bible it is referred to as "building up the body of Christ". You're fortifying your own spiritual identity by supporting and structuring, exerting and extending, joyfully and *willingly* creating this incredible learning experience for yourself, not trying to force it into existence.

Recognize that everything you are living now is the result of how you've used your will in the past. Vibration has longevity. So, what you'll live in the future depends upon what you choose to do with your spiritual will in the now. Don't be fearful of this fact — be grateful! This means you have the freedom to create as you wish. You are not victim of something outside yourself. Is this not a thrilling knowledge, a liberating wonder, to know that as you align yourself with higher intentions, moment by moment, that only goodness can follow? The highest use of will is to send forth the intention to follow the purest guidance available to you from your Team, guidance that comes both in the form of natural intuition and magnetically synchronized events. You are so familiar with your Team. You know them as well as you know the contours of your own face. So reach up to them with expectation.

Remember, a large portion of your soul still resides here with us. *Only a part of you is present upon the Earth.* It is this partial self that you are trying to integrate with your whole self. We are never far from each other in distance, substance, or awareness. If you can grow to truly understand that this is real, and allow it to unveil itself fully to you, you will have the delightful experience of seeing the most common of days infused with elevated insight and depth of meaning. And this, my dear ones, is what the Team aspires for you above all else!

You have in your hands a tremendous tool, this Will. Allow it to speak to your weaker aspects like a parent does a child, redirecting and guiding that energy into constructive avenues. It is the muscle aspect of your spiritual body, and your own powerhouse for change. Use it!

Everything is as real as you make it. You may direct the Will towards anger and make your anger the most powerful the world has ever known or you may direct your Will towards joy and make your life a fountain of mercy. You may direct your Will into illusions and they will seem more real than truth. Or you may direct your will towards truth, the story behind the story, and walk through the mists of illusion.

The world's fairy tales repeatedly tell the story of the use of willpower piercing the darkness of illusion. The prince cuts through the brambles around Sleeping Beauty's castle that no one has ever been able to penetrate. He uses a sword, his Will, driven by a sense of destiny and the power of love. The brambles are no match for his Will, and the illusion fall away. Once there, he finds all the castle inhabitants asleep from the spell of a witch. Recognizing this as yet another illusion, he presses on to the inner chamber of the castle where he is able to kiss the princess. With this kiss, not only the princess awakens — *everyone* awakens! His persistence, his realizations, has awakened his entire Team.

Each time you assert your spiritual Will, you enable others to awaken just a little more. You become a beacon in the fog of illusion. When those standing within the fog see this beacon, they realize it is not an impenetrable veil after all. They take hope that there is a Source for that light, and begin to move towards it. Therefore, when you meet people in despair or face a crisis of your own, speak your truth, as difficult as it might be. Words of truth are like the sword that cut down the brambles surrounding Sleeping Beauty's castle. They carry force, energy, power, and healing attributes. It takes courage to speak the words nobody would expect, to do the thing that is not usually done in the face of fear and sorrow.

Prepare yourself ahead of time to face these moments in life so you do not slip into predictable reactions of woe. I give you below some affirmations and quotes for this purpose. Rephrase them as you see fit. Make thoughts like these a part of your regular "spiritual vocabulary". Your use of them will open a door through which your Will may step, waving a torch of Light. Speak of this Divine Light when others are speaking of darkness, and you will alter the vibration of the conversation. For example, you might say:

- Let's stop a moment and draw closer to our Team
- Only a portion of our soul is here. The other part of us is on the Other Side, in total union with our loved one.
- That person was caught in a web of illusion to have acted in such a way.
- Our thoughts and emotions contribute to vast Vibrational Spheres of the same energy, which affect all of humanity. Let's contribute to compassion, not anger in this moment.
- I believe that Love will prevail.
- Our hearts are one. We can bear this together. Let's keep the faith.
- Angels are with her/him in this moment.
- He/she has a spiritual Team. He/she is not alone.
- We are just passing through this life. This is not a permanent condition.

- For every story of horror, there are millions of stories of goodness. Let's talk about those.
- If we have to confront this issue/person, let's do so with a voice of wisdom. Let's take the high road in this matter.
- Who do we want to be in this situation?
- This is our chance to walk the talk.
- Let's help each other act with dignity.
- Let's work as a team for the good of the all.
- I know the beautiful soul you really are, and that is what I to continue to see.
- I respect your free will.

CHILDREN

The experience of having parents and being a parent are two of the most instructional experiences of physical life. Ironically, as instructional as these experiences are, much greater insight is attained when we learn to *become unattached to our image of ourselves as parents and focus instead on who our children really are.*

When a child is born, we hold her gently in our arms, awash in our feelings of physical and emotional connection. It is such a wonderful, natural moment, one to be cherished forever. Imagine, however, the greater connection that would be possible in that moment if you were to look at that child and acknowledge that this entity, this beautiful soul, has come into a body out of its own volition, with its own spiritual Team, guardian angels and plans for this life. She's come into this family for a very, very special reason. She has a destiny. This is more than saying she has her "own path". It is to say that she has an entire legacy, both biologically and spiritually. She has brought all her unique spiritual and physical DNA to the forefront in that moment in time, right then, right at that instant. *Never before and never again will that particular combination of the two DNA's exist,* as expressed through that particular Time and Space event!

This event is truly far more precious and miraculous than anyone can possibly comprehend. Each child is one breath of God. Each new body contains matter that has existed in the Universe for eons of time, as well as a soul that is ageless, timeless, eternal, made in the image of God. Gaze upon your little one with these eyes, these thoughts, these emotions and she will feel your awareness of the treasure that she is. Do this regularly throughout your child's life, and loving respect will be the foundation you lay.

As you watch your child from the youngest of ages, bear in mind that you, as a parent, are a vehicle, a facilitator in a sense. You've come to this business meeting on the earth as a representative of a Team, and this child has done the same. And so, as the meeting unfolds, you begin to understand and communicate, soul to soul, what each one has brought to the table.

Your role in your child's life lies within the social structure of parenthood; however, the most important function you can fulfill in a child's life is that of a spiritual companion who recognizes who they really and who puts listening to their inner nature with all the questions, musings, and explorations which that involves, ahead of all other roles. Yes, when a child enters your life, you are being given the chance to build a connection that includes yet transcends traditional parenthood. You are being invited to be a spiritual mentor.

The beautiful thing about bringing this kind of awareness to your parenting is that is done completely through the power of your consciousness. No words are necessary, for if your realization of this fact is authentic, your child will feel and know that her *true essence, (not only her body and personality)* is adored, revered, recognized, treasured, supported, and applauded in every way. Verbal expression of it, while meaningful, is secondary. If you do this with your children, if you understand that this is the most refined role you can play and that your true calling is far beyond physical parenthood, you'll discover abilities within yourself that you never knew were there. Love and respect for another's spiritual path stirs up in us the best we have to offer. Specifically, it calls us to put the other's growth ahead of our own, and how we answer that call makes a huge difference in our own progress.

The day to day activities of caring for a child can easily cause one to get caught up in the details, forgetting the big picture. If you find yourself too caught up in the trappings of controlling your child's physical life, stop and remind yourself that your primary role is that of a spiritual friend rather than that of a gatekeeper.

Keeping those basic and necessary practical structures in place *while knowing they are secondary to this higher calling* is what makes parenthood such a tremendous opportunity for service and personal development. It is a chance to work daily on many important spiritual skills.

Becoming aware of when our ego is elbowing in our parenting is another way we learn from these relationships. Most of us believe we are pouring our essence out to our children, giving them everything we possibly can, straight from the heart. And while some of this outpouring arises from the most unselfish level of commitment, at times ego is the prevailing force.

It is easy to slip into the pattern of seeing our children as a reflection of how good a parent we are. We must keep watch for the raising of the ego-head all throughout our parenting. *We need only to recognize the presence of ego for positive changes to ensue.* Just sit back like someone on the sidelines and notice when thoughts arise such as, "I'm feeling this way because I think my children made me look bad," or "I'm feeling like a failure because I wish they'd done something different." Once you've seen an egoistic pattern of thought, ways to overcome that pattern will become evident to you. It is then that you must use your spiritual Will to counteract such thoughts in the future.

It's our mission to empower children from a young age to believe in their own ability to make choices. We may structure their time, but it's best to let them prove themselves right or wrong. In this way do we give them the chance to experience their creations firsthand rather than through some sort of hypothetical, contrived condition. By honoring the fact that they have a unique destiny and their own Team alliance, we allow them to develop their own spiritual "muscles," knowing that only resistance will strengthen those muscles. It's important to maintain a fundamental respect for the child's ability to choose, spiritually speaking, even if that means allowing errors to occur (within reason).

Indeed, parenting is a deliberate, careful dance between your sense of parental responsibility and your sense that these children are souls first with their own legacy and inner guidance, *united with our lives for a limited period of time and for a certain purpose.* Remember who they are, remember who they are, remember who they *really* are and by you remembering, you will activate a vibration that will radiate to them all they need to know about your intention for them. Having a deep, respectful awareness of their true identity, no matter how they're manifesting, will influence them far more than anything you say or do. Intention is everything. What people feel, what children feel, what anyone feels when they're anywhere near you is your vibration. It doesn't matter what you're saying, what you're wearing, or what you're doing… yes, those things can put up a temporary smokescreen, but at the soul level, what is activated, remembered, felt, sensed, and reacted to, is your central vibration. And children are more closely attuned to this than anyone.

The good news is that you can learn to control your central vibration! Take a few minutes per day to deliberately direct the love within your soul to the children in your lives. Then, when you see them, your reaction towards them will contain that same degree of buoyancy, hope, admiration, and respect. Without a doubt, they'll feel it from you, see it in your smile, and know it in the innermost part of their being. They will recognize that flash that fills your eyes that says, "There they are, those dear souls that chose me as their parent. How blessed I am to be able to participate in their path of discovery here on Earth." In that moment of soul-to-soul communication, your children will blossom a little more somewhere deep within themselves.

I always knew, when upon the Earth, who my children were and who they continue to be. I hope you always saw that my absolute adoration of you was because I held in my heart the vision of the "you" I know you were created to be. This upholding of the vision creates an eternal, unsullied, unbroken, happy, laughing, tender, powerful, all-knowing, all-feeling, all-forgiving net of acceptance that we can all rest in together. It creates a level of trust, honesty and surety that continues on through time, space, timelessness and spacelessness. It didn't mean everything we did was wise or everything you chose I supported, but *I knew that your purest essence would prevail*, for this is the way of the soul. Come what may, strive to hold that same vision for your children and your children's children, so that whatever happens in their lives, they will always have that same net of pure vision to lean back into.

Each one of you is working in a particular culture and environment that has its strengths and flaws. Life for children today is disturbingly tumultuous. There is an anchor missing, in a sense, but it can be restored by implementing a certain kind of structure. *Surprisingly, this structure is one of less, not more. Simplicity is what is needed.* Real one-on-one connection, relaxed conversations, and uncluttered time for reflection between family members and in the midst of Nature can heal a family faster than any system of therapy. The need for "therapy" however, can be greatly reduced if this simplicity is consciously embraced from the very start.

Begin with an infant in a relaxed environment, balanced carefully to avoid overstimulation, so the little soul can savor awhile longer her connection to the Absolute. What is the rush? Decrease impatient expectation of things and activities and you will automatically increase her connection to Nature, silence, play, beauty, imagination, and quiet observation. Let visual aesthetics and uplifting music be the norm, not the exception, in her young life. This is her time to lay a foundation! If peace is her foundation, all else that is good will follow.

Make a moment of prayer or meditation with the family the opening and the finishing of her day, the anchor between which all else occurs and all is reviewed. Seek out companions (both adults and children) who will bolster her sense of humor, of honor, of wisdom, of hope for a wonderful future. Developing that vision is essential, for if a child cannot look upward and see themselves in a state of joy, peace, achievement, and service, then in what direction are their eyes turning? They are either looking across a plateau that promises no progress or they are looking downward.

Teach her delayed gratification, for the ability to plant the seeds of creation and wait patiently and gratefully for the next phase of experience to come will be a blessing throughout her life. Do this in a playful manner, sharing grand visions of possibilities, drawing pictures with her of hopes and dreams, and then discussing the interesting journey that will be taken to achieve them. *Teach through example that there is joy in the journey, that it is not merely a hardship to be endured,* that there are many delightful moments along the way to the destination. Since a new destination will appear once that one has been attained, why fret that a certain goal is not instantly achieved? If it were to be suddenly achieved, the next logical step would just present itself anyway.

Help your little one see that every step of the journey is precious, not only the goal, and that her soul will be so greatly enriched when she learns to savor the now. Teach her to live in the now by appreciating the now yourself. And show her through the example you set with your words and actions, that very often the experiences that some people describe as undesirable or disappointing are often the richest in meaning. *Remember, she is watching how you respond to difficult times and will learn to imitate you perfectly.*

Older children's attitudes arise from either a lack or abundance of respect for the people in their lives. This respect cannot be forced or contrived. It's either real or it isn't. If it is, unrequested acts of thoughtfulness and care will characterize their behavior. If it isn't, there is only one thing to do. Provide these structures I've described of prayer and simplicity, and dissect your own behavior as to what example you are setting, to see if you are exemplifying what you wish them to mimic. Then, employ the tools of prayer to enshroud them with compassion and light. Pause and reflect throughout the day to remind yourself of who they really are, so that when you are together, they cannot help but feel this image radiating from your mind towards them.

Bring new contacts and experiences into their sphere that can act as a mentoring force beyond what you are capable of providing. *Call up the troops!* Talk to the Team, asking for assistance in inspiring these young ones to a state of respect for themselves, others, and their surroundings. You are not raising these children alone… there is a spiritual network of goodness available to you and to them.

One of the greatest antidotes to being overwhelmed by the responsibilities of raising children is to enter into the magical world of childhood yourself. Try to reconnect with your own youth — the state of mind you dwelled in, the curious perspective you viewed life from, the inner experiences you had that the adult world of rules and schedules had no connection to. Let your child be a child. Do not force upon her the fears, rigid viewpoints and prejudices of the world. Entice her into life's necessary rule-following with some games and lighthearted play.

Just as you delight in the infant's foolishness, delight in the older child's perspective as well, and enter into it with him. For if you have achieved an adult age, whether twenty, thirty, forty, fifty or more, within that number exist the infant, the toddler, the kindergartner, the teenager, and so on. *All those ages are within you still, and you can revisit them again!* Join her there from time to time, and in so doing show her that you respect her age, her stage in life, and her needs. *Prove to her that your world and your perspective is not the only one that matters.* Demonstrate to her that you value and appreciate her world as well. The truth is, young children are more connected to what is "real" than adults. Your slow and careful mindfulness of her "in the now" existence can teach you great things. *Stay aware of the fact that your children are your teachers.* Listen attentively to their lessons.

Give your child reachable standards, or her eager little heart will be perpetually frustrated. Remember that her most important task in this life is to discover that wellspring of spiritual light and joy within herself. Be sure you are not squelching that process of discovery in some way. *She is not your possession. She is on loan from the Universe.* Very likely, she is a member of your Team, or assigned to their guidance. Treat her as such.

Most of all, don't forget to laugh together! All great parents, like all great teachers, employ humor in their interactions with the young or the old. Laughter links you with a stream of vibration that is uniquely positioned to move straight to the heart. There is a reason you feel relaxed and energetic after you laugh — your body is responding to the beautiful vibration of joy. Laugh more than you lecture. Laugh more than you clean, plan, work or correct. Laugh more than you analyze, discuss, and organize. At times, let it all go — rules and all — and just laugh! Your children will be greatly blessed if you do and more likely to pass on a legacy of joy to the next generation.

ELIMINATION THROUGH ILLUMINATION

One of the main reasons we enter the Earth in the first place is to experience the illusion of Past, Present and Future. This linear view of Time helps us to see the pattern of cause and effect created by our thoughts and actions. By seeing this pattern, we grow to recognize the power we have to create causes and in turn, control effects.

It is as if a piece of putty has been stretched out from its original ball shape into an elongated piece of material so that you have more to work with. Along that elongated piece you can design markings that begin on one end and end at the other. In other words, you can create an image of Past, Present and Future on the putty. If you roll the putty back into one ball, the markings vanish, absorbed in the Now, the unified composite of all those markings. This "rolling up of the putty ball" is what occurs when you depart from your physical form and enter the Eternal Now.

You can do the same with a rubber band by stretching it out and writing a message on it that has a beginning and an end. Release the rubber band and it contracts, reducing the entire message to a small point. The very same information is there, yet it is occupying only a tiny space. Stretch it back out, and the message (the cause and effect) can be seen again.

Life upon the Earth is like the elongated putty or the stretched-out rubber band. You're living in a medium where things are slowed down, where events are rolled out one by one, so that you can watch them unfold and experiment with them through the illusion of Time. Days are divided into dark and light. Tasks are organized into ideas and completions. Physical changes are divided into stages spanning from infancy to old age. Seasons and weather patterns follow cycles. All of this exists to teach you how energy leads to more energy, words lead to more words, actions lead to more actions, thoughts lead to more thoughts, vibrations produce more vibrations, and that all of this is launched from within each of you.

You are the emissary of yourself that you have sent forth to the Earth to build up your spiritual muscles. You want the experience of seeing how principles work in slow-motion, so you have chosen to visit an energy field that is slowed down, the energy field of the Earth. To better comprehend this, imagine if you wanted to observe the sequence of events that are involved in producing a spark of electricity. You could watch a spark being generated a million times over and would never be able to separate the events well enough to see each of them in action. But film that process in process slow-motion, and you'd be able to observe each and every step involved.

Your environment and the body you are using are just like this — a slow-motion movie established to help you observe the functioning of spiritual principles. This slow-motion film is a gift to your soul, a chance for the effects of your vibratory decisions to become crystal clear to you. Once you have refined your experimental abilities so that you are conscious of the vibratory choices available to you, have recognized which ones you habitually choose, and have used your will to deliberately choose *the highest one available to you at any given moment*, you have learned one of the most important things the Earth has to teach you.

Looking at the Past is equal to looking at an originating thought, nothing more or less. Looking at the resulting circumstances of that thought is your big chance to comprehend the creative power you exercised when you launched that originating thought. Take hold of that chance-it is your greatest opportunity for growth. Grasping this is the key to understanding that the so-called "past" can be transmuted, as described before in the analogy of the font on a computer changing everything retroactively. This is not just feel-good theory, but a reality.

In keeping with this, we see that there is never any point in attacking the results of our past with more of the same that caused it. In other words, why react to our past anger with more anger? There is no point in warring *against* anything, for you are only adding more energy to what you wish to never repeat. The only way to uplift a condition is *by focusing upon the results you do wish to see.*

True transmutation never occurs through self-punishment, self-loathing, self-hatred or despair, which only heap deeper layers of negative vibration onto the very stage of development you wish to cleanse. Rather, it occurs when you become proactive, not merely reactive, in your deliberate selection of thoughts and actions that are expressions of Love, Will, and Grace through Legacy.

This process requires proactively sending forth rivers of pure intention. Throw this conscious awareness out as far as you possibly can, with all the force of your soul's will, like an Olympic champion tossing the discus with all his strength. This is the kind of passionate commitment needed to launch counteractive, transformative, healing energy.

To shake off lingering apathy and emotional fatigue, proclaim aloud and with determination, "I WILL create and respond with joy to every opportunity that appears in my life. I WILL encounter each fellow human being as an angel in disguise, with reverence and humility. I WILL teach what I have learned and learn as I teach. I WILL open myself to the guidance available from my Team, both those incarnate and discarnate."

It is this attitude, this dedication, this determination that will create a Light so brilliant that all the shadows of the past that haunt you will be absolutely eliminated through illumination. It's an avalanche that overpowers a valley. It is a hurricane that rearranges reality. It is a tidal wave that washes away all traces of what existed before. Your soul has the capacity to be as forceful as these elements, in relation to those things you choose to transmute. You have the tools in your own spiritual body, in your very own soul structure to achieve this. When unleashed in full array, nothing can stand in the way of the trinity of which you are comprised, a trinity made up of sparks from a most magnificent fire.

Those in the physical body underestimate their power to transmute, influence, and create. Many lives are only partially lived due to totally untapped resources and talents, which lead to the dimming of one's Light through apathy or discouragement. A great and heroic outpouring of the soul is needed, the kind of outpouring that you think of when someone rescues a person from a burning house. Hold high the vision of the discus thrower! Toss the disc of your greatest yearnings with all the belief and faith you can muster. Toss it into what appears to be the unknown, and you will soon find that it is not the "unknown" at all. Rather, it is the "inknown," the answer you are seeking, the fulfillment of all that you so deeply wish to manifest. A half-hearted toss will not do; it must be done with absolute abandon and commitment to go the distance. Once you have launched your discus, it will act as a comet streaking through the night, its tail burning up the lingering darkness behind it, and you will be free of what you call the Past, and ready to live, work, learn, and teach in the Eternal Vibratory Now.

JESUS

Knowing how important this subject is to so many people, I specifically asked my mother the question: "Is Jesus real?"Subsequent books elaborate further on the subject of Jesus, Lord of the Compassionate Heart.

Jesus was and is "real" in the broadest sense of that word. He is the representative of a band of consciousness infused with pure compassion. From this broad band come individualized expressions of the energies contained in that band, and so it was with the appearance of this person on the Earth.

He is regarded by many as the most important *type of consciousness* upon the Earth simply because there is such a tremendous need in your physical realm for the manifestation of his band's attributes: non-judgment, non-violence, hope, forgiveness, kindness, love, and reconciliation.

Those who follow him, *if they apply the essence of these principles*, will generate tremendous waves of love throughout the Earth. Those who use his image as a facade for acts of judgment and exclusion do the opposite.

Those who have had the experience of being ecstatically uplifted by the personage of Jesus are connecting to a ray of Light that his Team directs at the Earth. This Team is enormous, and is jubilantly and humbly united in their love for service to humanity. This beautiful offering, however, is filtered through so many people who are burdened by ego and personal agendas, that much of this pure outpouring becomes diluted and thereby misinterpreted. In its unsullied form, the essence of Jesus' ray provides a path which, if *followed in the manner which is intended*, is a path that leads straight to holiness and wholeness.

The symbolism of blood in connection with Jesus is a powerful one to his Team. He is said to have saved humanity through his blood, and people pray the blood of Jesus upon their lives. Look at the earthly parallel to this. What does the blood carry in your physical bodies? The answer is your DNA, your genetic heritage. Jesus' Team of Compassion, for that is what it is, works through Love to activate a follower's spiritual DNA. Jesus teaches that we are "saved by Grace" and are a part of the "body of Christ". What is this Grace and this collective body? It is your legacy, the third part of your spiritual body, a legacy that supplies assistance through grace to carry your soul to completion.

No one attains anything without this element of grace. Indeed, we are all "saved by grace," as Jesus proclaimed, not through literal blood, but through our spiritual blood, or DNA. The Universe operates on a system of unity, so none of us "go it alone" or "make it alone". In Book Four, this system of grace is described in detail as "The Absorbancy Principle," for absorbency of confusing energy that could overwhelm a soul is precisely what occurs when a wiser or stronger being assists another. Just as a frail person needs the physical assistance of a stronger one to cross over a swaying bridge, so does the soul need the assistance of his Team to take that final step across any significant threshold. It is this grace that supports us as we transition to our goal, and the personage of Jesus can activate this in many people. The key, as in all paths to growth, is not to allow attachment to any symbol or personality to become an excuse to express arrogance or fear. The Team of Compassionate Hearts that works with Jesus has nothing to do with such negative manifestations. "By their fruits ye shall know them."

Having said that, don't worry if someone chooses to pursue those kinds of manifestations, or any other limitations associated with religions, philosophies, or varieties of diversions for that matter. *All limitations are temporary and serve as useful transition steps.* Respect others' choices, remembering the necessity for all bands of consciousness and the natural asymmetric pattern to spiritual growth. Do not seek to control another's path, for it is pointless in the end. Be at peace, knowing that each person has their own Team behind them and will be guided, just as you are. You are not there to burst another's bubbles, only to seek out the highest truth you can grasp in your own life. Love is the only prevailing power, and all that is less than Love will be transformed eventually. Most certainly, the Team of Compassionate Hearts which Jesus leads is a most powerful part of that transforming process.

WHAT IS EVIL?

How well I know the burning desire to learn the answer to the question of what is evil. Collectively, you reel in horror at the cruel and violent events that occur upon the earth, and this horror yields a vibration, a steady hum of fear and bewilderment that is all around you there. I understand very well that feeling.

But from here, where all things appear as vibration and principles in action, I have a different perspective to share. I know that it will be a challenge for you to incorporate this view into your lives, because the sequence of choices that bring a person to the brink of evil's abyss is so lengthy, you seldom see the evidence of how that path develops and how it is ultimately reconciled. Here is what I now understand . . .

There is only one impulse in the soul… the impulse to expand consciousness. Everyone upon the Earth has this as his/her purpose, for no other purpose exists. Every soul has combined with a body knowing that the result will be access to the power of human ingenuity, an ingenuity that can be used to invent, create, and imagine. *The vilest of criminals and the most devoted of saints are both using this same vital life force to create with.* Whether they concoct evil plans or design compassionate programs for the poor, they are working with the same raw energy, just in very different ways. They each have hands with which to create, but choose to do the opposite thing from one another. They each have voices with which to speak, but use their voices in very different ways. They all have every kind of tool available to them, but choose to build very different structures.

The Earth's vibrations combine to make an incredible stew of kinds and sorts, the product of millions of years of this contrasting creative output. A soul's entry into this stew is a bit like entering a sea of very thick fluid. The Team has arranged for markers to lead the soul to a safe harbor, but each must rely on his own spiritual Will to follow these markers and make it there. The soul would not have it any other way, any more than a young adult wants to be forever coddled and carried through life's storms.

By entering into this "sea," the soul is taking his chances with the rest of humanity that he will be sufficiently reactive to the magnetic pull of the markers that his Team has placed in the Earth, markers designed to beckon him to safety, markers that are designed to guide his destiny. The soul has agreed that he will blend with humanity for this time, knowing that all the challenges and illusions inherent in that decision are going to become part of his temporary reality. He knows he will have to be crafty and careful to invite only the highest he is capable of aligning with, while still allowing himself to taste of the many experiences the world has to offer. He also knows that in order to become empty of ego, he will first have to know fullness; in order to become light, he will have to encounter the darkness, in order to be non-violent, he will have to witness violence, in order to know the depths of forgiveness, there will have to be something to forgive. All this requires a tremendous amount of weighing and balancing the many aspects of life.

Clearly, some people do not find the pattern of the markers left for them to follow. Instead, they get lost in illusion, and like the mythical character who is lured by the sea's goddesses into deeper and deeper waters, they wander too far away to hear the voices of his Teammates. There are many degrees of this wandering. Some are slight diversions, which are quickly corrected. These kinds of diversions provide a healthy dose of contrast that serves the soul well. Some are more intense diversions, which take much more effort to correct. And others are deep and wide diversions that take many lifetimes to create and much schooling to resolve.

Envision these diversions as a jungle full of vines. If you choose to swing on vines that are even just a millimeter higher than the last, you will without a doubt eventually have to arrive at your ultimate destination — the treetops. One vine lower, though, and you will encumber yourself, or at best stay at the same level. Twenty vines lower, and you may hit the ground. Swinging back up, this time with a broken arm and leg, will be a totally different experience than it could have been.

All of these diversions are based upon the soul's strength of will or lack of it, his identification with ego, and his openness to humility. Humility is the recognition of one's proper place in the Universe. It is not self-condemnation. *In fact, self-condemnation or self-loathing is a form of pride*, for it is based upon the special idea one has about oneself, that unlike everyone else, one "should" be above making mistakes. Humility, on the other hand, is the recognition that we all can make these mistakes, and that we are no different, (i.e., no better and no worse) than anyone else. It's the great leveler, and once experienced, it actually relieves a person of the unreasonable and painful expectation of personal perfection. It is said in Paul, "I was given a thorn in the side so I might not boast..." Accept that the human experience is meant to contain a certain degree of contrast and friction (thorns) to help you feel connected to everyone else's experiences.

Humility paves the soul's way home. Without it, involvement in the lower vibrations of Earth life only increases. The slide into these vibrations is rarely rapid; it is incremental. Alignment with great evil does not occur in a flash, even though it may appear to do so. *It develops slowly as one stubbornly persists in the embrace of illusion.* Every conceivable life raft is offered in every imaginable form in an effort to redirect a struggling soul. The greatest of these life rafts was placed by God in a place we can always find it — the entire world of Nature. Every aspect of Nature is a reminder of the glory of Truth, and this beauty is ever calling out to us. The sunrise and sunset that appears every single day has enough wisdom, light, hope, and promise in it to guide our entire spiritual journey if we would but let it. But there are those who close their eyes to those things that were placed in their path to inspire them, and their alignment with lower Vibrational Spheres begins to outweigh the higher alignment.

Everything is done by the Team to lift someone out of this state, but the natural flow of information back and forth between him and the Team becomes so clogged, it is eventually limited to droplets that quickly evaporate.

To rally from the miasma he has entered, this lost soul attracts to himself a stricter Law, enacted to reveal to him the condition he is in. He commits an act of horror, an act that is the culmination of the many lives he has chosen illusion over truth. This vile act is his total commitment to the darkness he has embraced, and results in an explosion of the dynamite he has so carelessly toyed with for so long. It is an act he cannot hide from, one that causes the illusionary world to which he has joined himself to literally blow up in his face.

I know it is hard to comprehend, but this turmoil has stemmed from the same basic impulse that caused another person to become a beacon of light for the world… the two have simply pointed their creative power in completely opposite directions. Those who are affected by the vile act of this person are very often Teammates who have agreed to play a part needed to shake up and wake up their companion. In some cases, a very advanced soul agrees to "absorb" the darkness of this lost soul by playing that role for them.

The Team now has a broken soul in its membership, a soul that finally calls out from beneath the rubble of darkness with a sincere and humble cry for help, a soul who sees the world of illusion for what it's not worth, ready to heed his Elders, compensate those he has hurt, and use the tool of his personal energy for a higher purposes. The Team will not forsake him, and thus begins the painful process of assisting him in the climb upward he must now make.

Much of this climb occurs upon the Earth, but in the case of such a "fall," the review on the Other Side holds profound impact. Once here, he is shown the results of his negative choices from the perspective of others *as well as the alternative results that might have been.* The contrast between the two is so immense, the soul is filled with the deepest of longings to re-enter the Earth and cleanse it of the low vibratory markers he has left behind. Subsequent incarnations may be characterized by acts of extreme, even heroic goodness that appear out of nowhere in a person who seems troubled in every other way. This is a sign that a soul and its beloved Team are striving together to make good on their commitment to balance the scales.

Many of the most passionate workers upon the Earth in the fields of human rights, animal rights, ecology, spirituality, healing, counseling and the like, are those very ones who are determined to change the vibratory conditions of the negative situations they were participants in before. In the fullness of Time, such a soul can attain great heights, but first he must struggle to rise one mere increment above where he now lies, and work through the bands of consciousness he once might have flown through — a grueling process.

In summary, horrific acts of evil are the extreme form of the natural explorations of the soul, *a form that is the exception rather than the norm.* It is the result of *long-term alignment* with the lowest vibrations available in the "sea," occurring not in a brief moment but throughout many lifetimes. Long-term alignment of this kind puts an individual in league with warped Vibrational Spheres of collective anger and confusion, spheres created by the focus of a multitude of thoughts throughout time. In this way, a weak impulse towards negativity is linked up with a larger impulse, and the intensity of the emotions and compulsions that result are overpowering. In other words, the lost soul's smaller wave of negativity finds alliance with other similar waves, and he becomes caught in a virtual tsunami of destruction *far beyond anything he could have been capable of creating if he'd only been acting solo.* Keep in mind that evil actions are fueled by collective evil, just as benevolent actions are fueled by collective good.

For all these obvious reasons, your Team beseeches you who read these words to remain humble, to use your Will to build up the Christ nature in yourselves and others, to observe and to *truly listen* for direction. The Team is always ready to interact with you, if only you will acknowledge them, ask for their assistance and collaboration, and then be willing to watch for what answers come your way. As you go out into your day, strive to recognize that all around you are pulsating impulses and items created through human ingenuity, that unique product of the combination of body and soul. From the most exquisite painting to the littlest child's scribble, from the simplest hut to the most elegant statue, from the bustling cities to the quiet villages, learn to recognize them all as results of this urge to create. This urge is filtered, and cannot be as pure in manifested form as in ideated form, but nonetheless, this is what it is.

Likewise, look at each person and recognize *that at the soul level, they are seeking what you are seeking — spiritual expansion — nothing more and nothing less,* no matter who they are or what they are doing. The human mind innately knows this is so, and weaves symbols of this fact into the fabric of everything in the world. This is why the *free will choice of the soul* is described in every myth, fairy tale, legend, and holy book around the world. You can be an agent of assistance to people who are involved in this steady slide towards Vibrational Spheres of darkness. Send out a prayer to everyone you meet, from one soul to another, that they quickly recognize their particular masks of illusion and make the higher choice of whatever vibrations they happen to encounter. This simple formula, just choosing the highest out of a set of given choices, will yield incredible results. Be determined to see the light in everyone you meet, for oftentimes just the fact that someone recognizes that light can lead one out of illusion.

Believe in them, as we believe in you. Believe that they will listen to their Team and their inner guidance for their own sake and the sake of all humanity. *Send forth encouragement, for the conditions upon the Earth are collectively created, and another's state of being does affect your path, just as yours affects theirs.* As pointed out before, your vibratory offerings of love and light are swept up and duplicated beyond your wildest expectations; and in this way are they your greatest tool to helping yourself and others avoid the pitfall of alignment with evil.

PROTECTION

As you maneuver through the temporary structure of the Earth experience, the instinct for protection arises. This instinct is a necessary component for the physical body to survive. It is an innate impulse for self-preservation, shared by all living things. If it were not so, physical life and the marvelous opportunities it offers to the soul would be cut short. Certainly, this would not bode well for preserving the valuable school of Earth and the bodies that you now utilize. But let us focus now not on physical protection, but spiritual.

There is one main thing we should seek to protect ourselves from during our journey through life: the false mask of pridefulness, which is the originator of the majority of all other illusions. When pride gets its foot in the door, things begin to shift from the real to the ephemeral. This can occur so slowly and incrementally, one is not aware of the change. Eventually, one finds oneself far from the source, bewildered by the twisting turns of a labyrinth.

The pride referred to here is not when we are pleased with the positive effects of our work, family, or other accomplishments, but rather when we are caught up in arrogance built upon the desire to control illusionary elements believed to give one self-worth. Some of these elements include over-identification with one's appearance, status, physical belongings, and even one's creative, intellectual or spiritual development. It is possible to feel pride over almost anything one chooses, including a sense of "not belonging," "difference," or "specialness". All of this leads away from the truth of unity into the illusion of separateness. *Always remember that pride divides, humility unites.*

A mighty river flows as one unit, consisting of many droplets that exist to serve the purpose and uphold the direction of the river. Pride creates numerous blockages, resulting in detours in our stream of spiritual contact. Just small rivulets form around obstacles to the river's flow, so do our divine intentions become sidetracked and delayed when we mistake these lesser routes for our actual course. One distraction leads to another, causing us to wander aimlessly, all the while believing we are right on target. At times, the experience of becoming lost is so complex that we enter into a full encounter with the lowest of vibrations. This causes great suffering, both collective and personal. It is a spiritual experience equivalent to the physical experience of going blind and requires a tremendous effort to heal.

This process is described in the Biblical story of the prodigal son who, after many years of painful wandering in search of fulfillment, returns to his father's house where he is wholly accepted. As beautiful as this story is, we must remember that the circuitous path chosen by this son produced huge challenges for those involved. Each detour required correction. As the son struggled, the father waited, pushing through his pain with love, keeping the candle lit in the window, striving to keep the flames of hope alive. The father could not do for the son what needed to be done. He could only hold high the lantern of inspiration and loyalty. The son could not do for the father what he had to do, either. He was overwhelmed with the task of digging out from beneath the layers of delusion he had previously so eagerly embraced. The choices of one grieved many, but it did not have to be so.

There is a less painful way, and from my perspective beyond the body, I see it clearly. For this reason do I speak to you now from my heart with great hope for your own progress, of the possibility of moving into a state of consciousness we might call "a willing return" so your path may bring you and those you reach more ease, more laughter, more depth of compassion. Yes, you have come to the Earth to explore, to sample the smorgasbord of life. But in every restaurant there are chef's recommendations and waiters' suggestions! In the same way, your Team's guidance is valid and can lead you to a more delectable experience.

While a certain number of these stream-like wanderings are a natural part of our evolution, causing us to yearn to return to the greater flow, there comes a time in one's development that these wanderings and their inherent lessons simply hold no more appeal... *a time when we are willing to look squarely at everything in our experience and unveil the mystery behind the facade.* It is a time when our desire to be a vessel of light overrides our desire to preserve the precious illusions we have embraced. If you are reading this, now is that time for you.

How am I to recognize this pride, you may ask?

Pride is at the root of all other illusions. It is that element that causes one to judge another, to punish another, and to do the same to ourselves. It is that element that causes one to think, "I've got mine, you go get your own." It is that element that causes us to undermine another person through words, thoughts, or deeds. It is that element that causes us to cry "I *deserve* better," rather than "I *am capable* of creating better."

Pride is that element that causes us to want to instruct more than we want to learn, to be respected more than we respect, to be known rather than to know, to be given a seat and served at the table of honor rather than recognizing that the servant is the greatest teacher. It is that element that causes us to think we should receive what we have not earned, to hoard what we do not need, to be dissatisfied with the blessings that we have, and to resent lessons that involve humility. Pride sucks the joy out of our lives. It inserts hesitation and inhibitions into our expressions of love and vulnerability. As we become swept up with the newest illusion, pouring our thoughts and time into it, we find that it's a dead-end and we must backtrack, reconsider, and rebuild.

This cycle of expectation and disappointment is due to attachment, which is the gluey substance secreted by pride. To counter such attachment, ask yourself, how would it feel to simply be a "regular" person? What, indeed, is a "regular" person? Truth be known, there is no such thing. Every life is a rare and intricate mixture of vibrations infused with a surprising personal history. Seeing the most ordinary of lives for the absolute miracle that they really are — this is the key to contentment.

Every seeker eventually discovers that operating from a place of pure intention *without any concern for the results of that intention* is the way to protect oneself against the illusions born of pride. Stating "I intend to commune with my Team and reflect that communion in my actions and words" is a pure intention. Stating "I intend to commune with my Team so I may obtain something I desire," is a strings-attached intention. While strings-attached efforts may produce some results, they are often at the expense of the more refined result that could have been created through pure intention.

Strive to launch your intentions from the purest, simplest point within yourself, holding no preconceived results in mind. This is the way to know that what you're creating is for the highest good, both yours and others. Instead of seeking the power of persuasion, seek to have a voice of truth. Instead of seeking superiority, seek the spirit of honesty. Instead of seeking cleverness in the marketplace, seek to be a beacon of goodwill and generosity in the public arena. From the humblest heart great things are created.

Freedom from pride unleashes a level of energy and enthusiasm that is not dependent upon outer conditions. On the contrary, pride often produces spiritual indifference, for it causes an imbalance between the grace we have received and our manifestation of that grace. Basking in the beauty of our new awareness, we can become indulgent and lazy. This is not to be confused with the periodic breaks that occur within lifetimes (i.e., the spiritual equivalent of "a second cup of coffee"), for to everything there is a season. There is a natural ebb and flow to how we comprehend a new degree of truth, absorb it, express it, and absorb it again at a deeper level. This is different from the feelings we have when we've neglected the development of important spiritual attributes, disregarded opportunities to uplift others and are talking the talk without walking the walk.

If you are completely committed to using this lifetime for the highest possible purpose, this apathy must be opposed by your Divine Will. One of the first thought patterns that need adjusting is the concept that you possess anything of a physical nature. Everything is "on loan" from the Universe, including the stardust in your body. Any talent, beauty or strength you have is not uniquely yours. It belongs to the creative force that fashioned it. You are given it to use temporarily so that you may complete a certain phase of existence. Even the wisdom you attain in this life will eventually be merged into vast Vibrational Spheres of specialized energy available to all. It will not remain "yours" alone, but will be shared freely.

All of creation is collective; therefore, you do not and cannot "own" anything. This acquisitive manner of thinking causes a condition you may consider as "spiritual indigestion," and it is as miserable as the physical condition! Spiritual paralysis is a real condition too, caused by too little use of one's spiritual hands and legs. There is practical work to be done in the field of spiritual service, and until your Truth is put into action, your awareness is nothing more than the "painting in your head" that has yet to find its way to the canvas to inspire anyone. "Elbow grease" is required in one's spiritual life just like it is required in physical life, if our creations are to truly shine. Therefore, commit your energy to the polishing of true diamonds, not paste jewelry. It takes a large amount of energy to keep an illusion alive. On the other hand, truth requires no artificial "propping up," for it is supported quite literally by the wings of the Universe.

The great impulses of your heart to comfort humanity and to create uplifting conditions on the Earth are your guiding light. Follow them, and banish with carefully chosen spoken affirmations those grey mists of apathy. Refuse to let those mists define you. Choose instead that vibrant and passionate self that you have encountered along the way, the one that enlivens all that it comes into contact with. You know it well, but have yet to harness it and make it your habitual and consistent offering. Take charge of your will, speaking to the weaker parts of your nature as a firm parent speaks to a child. Speak aloud to yourself! Spoken words have power, for they are nothing more than pure vibration. Make words your ally. Speak into existence what you wish to manifest, but speak of only pure intention, unattached to results or desires.

So much emphasis has been placed on manifesting changes in physical conditions through the power of thought, but this is only the outer shell of this body of teachings. If you wish to access the more esoteric wisdom, "Seek first the kingdom of God, and all else will be added unto you." Suspend your interpretation of what "all else" means, and simply seek first that kingdom. You can then be certain that you are working from a divine place and that what comes as a result of it is a divine product, not a contrived one.

You may decide that it's necessary to halt all outer projects that you have in motion as you focus for a time on the purification of your motives before returning to those projects. In other words, it may be necessary to re-examine the entire foundation of your life to make sure your underlying motives are in keeping with your Team's essential mission. Don't let fear stop you from this process. If you hold fast to your commitment, the support you need will eventually manifest itself. What appears to be delay does not mean defeat. It is simply part of the process of reassessment and reconstruction.

Remain confident that your Team can see the broader scope of your path, and hearken to their signs and directions.

When you do begin anew, you may find that previous projects no longer hold appeal for you, or that they've branched out into unusual, or even unrelated directions. The apple cart may appear to be upset for a while, but all will eventually be righted. And when this occurs, celebrate whatever it leads you to. At least you will know that you are walking in harmony with the true Light.

Peace of mind is the ultimate goal... not the fragile peace of earthly security but the lasting peace of purely aligned intentions. Better to be a peaceful laborer than a frazzled jet-setter. The opposite must be said, too. Better to be a peaceful jet-setter than a frazzled laborer! The outer form is not relevant-it is the degree of inner authenticity that creates the quality of your life. It is this authenticity I am encouraging you to develop in yourself, for in such a rarified atmosphere, false pride cannot survive.

It's important to add here a reminder to stay emotionally and physically balanced during the process of recognizing and neutralizing pride. Wild extremes may yield results temporarily, but they will not be long lasting. In fact, such excesses may become convenient excuses, providing distractions under which you may hide. Respectfully take care of your body with necessary rest and foods, but do not overindulge it. Remember what it is — a vehicle you have chosen through which you can apply what you have learned. Neglecting it will cause you to have to interrupt your work to repair it. Indulging it will also cause an interruption, for either one of these excesses cause illness. Acknowledge your body with gratefulness for the service it provides, and apologize if you have abused it, vowing to provide better care.

Pride will also interfere with the natural, balanced blend of meditation, work, pleasure, healthy self-care, and service to others.

When we are busy with the exhausting task of chasing pipe dreams, valuable things fall to the wayside. When we are rooted in eternal values, it is virtually impossible to neglect them.

Each of these things must be looked at with blinders off, but as you examine your life for the element of pride, please do not despair. Your goal is to recognize this trait the instant it arises, but entering into depression when you see it is tantamount to a child on a ball team throwing a temper fit when he misses the ball. The thought, "I am too good to lose. I am supposed to always catch the ball. Others can miss it, but not me!" is *not* a drive towards excellence but yet another form of pride. Why would you think that you and you alone are capable of perfection, while others are destined to flounder? Accepting your own shortcomings with the same tender spirit that you direct at others' shortcomings is the highest evidence of true humility. *It proves that you fully understand that you are no greater and no less than any other being.*

Pride is the thorn in the side of every human being, and recognition of it is the great refiner. It will always be present. Therefore, do not expect it to vanish, but on the contrary to show itself to you more and more. As you grow, you will notice it everywhere, both in yourself and in others. This increase in recognition is evidence of progress; therefore, be joyful when you discern it, not discouraged! It is not increasing; only your *awareness* of it is increasing. So, like a child who finds another child playing hide-and-go-seek, say, "Ah-ha, gotcha!" and simply chase it away. And, as children always do, be sure to laugh for as long as you can at yourself and your fleeing foe, for laughter is truly the best medicine, even (and perhaps especially) in spiritual matters.

INERTIA

Inertia is the "drag" in any given situation, the opposing force that causes the achieving force to push harder to complete its task. This principle is well-known in science, and as you surely see, science and spirituality are partners. Much of Earth life appears to involve correcting, cleaning, organizing, discarding, and tearing down, all for the purpose of using, rearranging and building up again. Consider how much time is used each day in these processes, from the simplest action of washing a dish to the huge projects of constructing a city. All of this is a balance between inertia and the achieving force.

Inertia is a relative principle. What is heavy and unbearable to you may be another person's highest achievement! Likewise, what is acceptable to you might be considered to be such an intense form of friction for another person that they fall into depression. Why is this so? Because inertia is caused not by any real condition, but by your ego! It is caused by your assessment of a situation as it relates to your reputation, your image, your fears and your cultural expectations. The heaviness that you feel coming upon you when you imagine certain scenarios in life as they relate to your comfort or success is an "illusionary thought entity." If you were to think about this same scenario from the standpoint of another culture or another collection of life experiences, you may not feel any heaviness whatsoever. For example, one person might embrace the idea of living in a tipi, while another person could regard this as the ultimate humiliation and misery.

The Fortune 500 company president has a different definition for "financially strapped" than does a homeless person. A fashion designer has a different definition of "dressed poorly" than does a person who delights in thrift shop purchases. A hungry person has a different definition of what tastes good than does a restaurant critic. The parent of a disabled child has a different definition of educational milestones than does the parent of a genius. Each of these situations carries its peculiar brand of inertia, a brand that could be disintegrated instantly by a change of consciousness.

There is no right or wrong to this concept. There is simply the fact that all heaviness, resistance, sense of disappointment, sense of boredom, sense of limited resources, and so forth is coming from the gap between your *definition* of something and what you are living. It is an imaginary experience, and one that you can learn to control rather than allowing it to control you.

This is not to say that you shouldn't have aspirations for more wonderful manifestations in life, but those aspirations can either be a stone around your neck or a springboard to joy. Simply recognize that the conditions you are now living in would be, to scores of people, their most cherished vision of wellbeing, the most beautiful condition that they can possibly imagine. Look at your condition and know that it is a condition of great worth and value in relation to the whole. Cease all complaining about any condition you are experiencing, physical or otherwise, and embrace it for the gift that it is. By doing so, you remove the inertia you have attached to it and are released to create something greater.

I encourage you to question your self-created experiences of inertia when they come upon you. Simply question them, without acting upon them any way. Ask yourself, "How is my *perception of this situation* contributing to the inertia that I am feeling?" You might find that the clash between your feelings and your ego-based idea fades away when challenged.

Imagine a runner who wishes to achieve a certain speed. It is possible for him to become so involved with the attaining of that speed that he descends into a spiral of despair over his current speed. This despair can trigger his immune system to overload, causing greater drag on his running speed. All the while, other runners consider his speed their ultimate goal, and would be elated to attain it.

If the runner could release his despair over his current speed and see what a treasure it is in the big picture, he would become strong again and, when he least expects it, attain that next speed. Interestingly, when he does he might realize, as do many people once they've attained a certain goal, that it's not as fulfilling as he thought it would be. The reason for this is because once he arrives there through appreciation for what he is currently living, it will feel different from what he had expected. For one, he will have learned that while it is indeed a wonderful thing to run at such a speed, in the larger picture it actually embodies the very same principles he has discovered and directed in other situations. Secondly, he will have lived it so many times in his mind that it will not be as new and startlingly fresh as he'd predicted.

Therefore, in many ways it is best not to over-plan or over-visualize your next step. Spend the majority of your time reveling in the wonder of where you now are, and a part of the time loving what is coming next, without describing it in too much detail. Let it arrive packaged as a surprise!

The importance of understanding this cannot be underestimated. It is truly your key to being at peace with your current conditions while you continue to better your life. Take some time to assess *with great honesty* your physical environment, your health, your relationships, and your talents and bask in the beauty of them, whatever they are, for they represent the peak of some level of achievement. By treasuring them, and treating them with reverence, you will release the inertia you have attached to them and catapult yourself to a new experience.

If you are living in one room, make that room the most lovely, peaceful room that you can. See it as the blessing that it truly is, knowing full well that many do not have even one room of their own. If you are living with one arm, know that many have lost both arms, and treat that part of your body with utmost appreciation. If you are working in a difficult environment or for low pay, recognize that this place has much to teach you, and do your job humbly and well. When you do leave it, do so with respect and honor. If you are in a painful relationship, bless that relationship for what it has to teach you, and it just might transform before your very eyes. Or, if you decide to leave the relationship, do so with kindness and honesty.

A wise practice upon departing any person or place is to perform a simple ceremony (either in your mind or using actions) designed to thank and bless the experience that you've had (whether painful or beautiful) before moving on. This can be a simple as a moment of silent honoring to as complex as the lighting of a candle and the utterance of a prayer… what you are after is a spirit of reverence and appreciation, which will automatically infuse your next experience with the same energy. Remember, *what you do in the smallest areas of your life transfers to the largest areas of your life.* Therefore, thinking and acting with respect towards seemingly insignificant things will drastically alleviate the drag of inertia when the big things come along.

Don't be surprised when this inertia lifts, your vision for what you wish to create anew has changed as well, for you will be looking out over the vista from a fog-free pinnacle, seeing things you never even knew existed. If this occurs, be willing to release your previous "highest" aspiration, lest you bog it down again with ego-formed inertia. You just might leap into a level of possibilities that surpasses anything you have previously envisioned.

TRANSIENCY

The temporary nature of all Earth forms, be they plant, animal, mineral or human, is a source of fear for most people. This fear arises for two reasons: because people so closely identify with their bodies and what they can touch and see in their environment that they block awareness of their ongoing broader existence, and because the human body, in order to continue on Earth, carries with it an intense survival instinct which manifests as the impulse to cling to the familiar.

Here are two concepts about transiency which I hope can relieve some of your fear:

First, nothing is really gone. Everything is eternally in existence on some plane. What happens to make it appear transient is that your focus, combined with the focus of others, shifts. It is your focus that is transient, not the original ideation of the object of your focus. So what appears to be loss is actually a shift in focus, either another person's focus or yours, or both of you.

One example of this is love relationships. When a couple focuses upon one another in the most attracted of ways, there is what they call "being in love". When one or both shift their focus away from that bond, the bond changes. The change has come about due to a shift in focus, not the death of the essence of Love, which is eternal.

Consider the most prominent example of transiency-physical death. Death is simply the shifting of a soul's focus from the earthly body to another plane. This redirection of energy allows the physical body to cease its functioning. The vestige of that person continues to exist in ideation on another plane. It simply has no focus to hold it in its current circumstance and vibration.

The death, or change, has come about because of a shift in focus, not the death of the essence of Life, which is eternal.

The appearance of a limited longevity is build into all earthly forms, so that, as said before, the linear progression of cause and effect can be witnessed. It is focus that is shifted to bring about these changes, these various kinds of beginnings and endings-but change is not equivalent to loss. Everything is eternal in essence, even when it is transmuted into a higher degree. Within the 100-year old man are the infant, child, teenager, young man, and middle aged man. They have all combined to make the 100-year old man, and he contains the essence of each one of them. We look at the aged one and say he has lost his youth, when in truth he contains the essence of all the youth he has ever possessed. Therefore, the aged one is not bereft of youth; he is instead a composite of everything he appears to have lost.

Secondly, you only exist upon the Earth in part. You are your own reflection, and an extension of your Team. You have willingly embraced the Earth for the "hands in the clay" experience and to watch the "slowed-down parade of cause and effect" opportunity it offers, but have no doubt, the "you" that is still here at the table with us knows full well that there is no loss of Love or Life. It is very much like how you divide your personal life from your career life. At work, you have a certain persona that is conducive to getting the job done. At home, your hobbies and personal relationships are what you consider much more the "real" you. Yet even while you are working through the "work persona," this "real" you is still present, and vice versa. Similarly, on the Earth, an extension of you is in work mode, using a certain persona to learn lessons and grow. On the Other Side, your essential self continues to brim over with spiritual vitality. This vitality is pouring towards your work persona, infusing it with energy and passion. To the degree that you learn to incorporate and balance the work mode persona and the essential self will you bring the best of who you really are into the workshop of life.

This is the Great Work-accepting the infusion of energy from both your Teammates and the higher portion of yourself, choosing how to apply this combination of forces to any given situation, and supporting the entire process with Love, Will and Grace through recognition of your Legacy. Never forget that at all times the Team is pouring their essence into you, supporting and enriching your Earth experience. Understand that the Earth and the Other Side overlap, and that you exist in both places, not as a divided entity but as a whole entity that has chosen to place *some of your focus* on the Earth. You are not separated from us or from this greater part of yourself. You are not separated from the Team. Simply choose to be aware of this, to accept this fact, and you will see tremendous changes in your perspective of yourself, others, and the Earth. Remind yourself from time to time that nothing is really gone and you are only partly there, and this will help you keep the concept of transiency in perspective.

EXTRAPOLATION

I see from here that the simplest things upon the Earth represent the most glorious things in my midst. An earthly sunset is caused by refracted Light, just as it is here. An earthly piece of music is based upon the same principles of vibration that music is built upon here. An earthly body functions as does a spiritual body, with processes of absorption, comprehension, and transmission. In other words, our worlds mirror one another; how could it be otherwise, since there is only one Universe?

In my present form, I am an extrapolated being, while you are an interpolated being. Neither of these conditions is superior nor inferior to the other and both are temporary, for change is always just around the corner. There are many kinds of births and deaths involved in moving from one dimension to another, not only upon the Earth.

Just as the Other Side includes full perception of your state, so can you from your side perceive to a degree the way things manifest here. The purpose of your striving for this perception is not to escape where you are or what you are doing, but to better *know the sanctity of your own life!*

Your world, as experienced through your senses, can become a holy and mystical experience through the principle of extrapolation. All that is required is the deliberate and conscious choosing of it. The most menial task can become, if you so choose, a pathway to bliss through this profound and simple principle.

Each and every day, take a segment of time to develop the skill of extrapolation, and eventually it will become your automatic response to the job of living. Sit, walk, and observe your environment in the following manner. Each time you do this, your experience will change, because there are infinite levels to which a concept may be extrapolated.

1. Still the mind and body and breathe deeply, with the conscious awareness that physical breathing is a microcosmic form of receiving the sustenance of Truth from your Team. Breathe in reception of all that your Team has to offer. Breathe out to share what you have received. Your breath is now a symbol of a divine principle. You have expanded, or extrapolated, the meaning of your own breathing.

2. Look upon solid items, from furniture to buildings, and envision in your mind's eye the vibrations of energy that comprise those objects. Know that they are simply waves of thought that are held in a certain formation for a certain purpose, and that in an instant, they could disassemble and disappear. They are transient, as are your bodies. Their power lies not in what they appear to be but what they represent. You have now extrapolated the meaning of physical objects.

3. Walk slowly through your neighborhood or yard. Notice the details of Nature, from shades of color to texture, scents and sounds. Recognize that each step you take is a symbol of spiritual progress. Notice the various stages of growth or decay you see within Nature, and understand them to be symbols of the cycles of life and death, ascension and rebirth. Gaze upon each flower as the fruit of the soul, listen to each note of the birds' song as a message from the divine. You have now extrapolated a moment in Nature.

4. Look into a mirror, into your own eyes, at your own countenance. Drop your preconceived notions of yourself and instead see yourself as a stranger, as an alien might see you. Observe your body as if it belongs

to someone else. Strive to remove all identification of your true self from your body, and to the best of your ability, suspend any sense of admiration or rejection of the body. Acknowledge that the body you are using is a tool for the purpose of strengthening the Will, expressing the Love, and activating Grace through the Legacy of your spiritual body. It is a vehicle through which you may exercise human ingenuity. Appreciate it, care for it, but have no illusions about it. It is not you. You are a radiant being of Light whose aura extends far beyond the confines of your body. Everything about your body symbolizes an aspect of your soul. Take the time to think about each organ of the body and how it operates. How might these symbols relate to the grander scheme of life? How might they help you to better comprehend the heartbeat of humanity, the mind of God, the purification of the soul, the elimination of illusionary thoughts, the balance of duality, the filtering of impurities from one's being? You have now extrapolated the meaning of your own body's functioning.

5. Immerse yourself in water. Move yourself in the water, and closely watch the water as it ripples over your body. Imagine if you had never seen water before-what a miraculous element it would appear to be, as it drips and shimmers across you. Look how you can move through it, almost as easily as moving through air. How would you describe this to an infant, or to a being from another planet? In the same way, I can hardly describe to you the rarified medium through which I am moving now. Water is your closest parallel. You have now extrapolated the meaning of water.

These are only a few examples of how taking the time to objectively view yourself and your environment can vastly expand your comprehension of the greater principles at work throughout the Universe. Your world is not humdrum. Your world is not tedious or restrictive. It is brimming with symbolism, reflection, and information about how the Universe works-both the inner and the outer realms. This information is not under lock and key. You have been endowed with a natural capacity to fathom the true meaning behind each aspect of your world, thereby transforming the simplest acts of life into sacred rituals designed to lift your soul to heights of liberation. Therefore, it is possible for you to learn to extract infinite joy and purpose out of a single breath, and to convey this precious insight to others.

One of the greatest results of this practice is the development of a sustaining faith. Once you have attained the ability to look at a droplet of water and intuit the concept of an ocean, you will transfer this surety to many other parts of your life. Indeed, your life will become a series of extrapolations. The mere act of opening a door, driving to a destination, swimming in the sea, rocking an infant, sharing a meal, climbing a tree, swinging in a swing, writing on paper, playing an instrument, dancing, drawing, playing a sport, planting a garden, *of simply living*, will become representative of eons of ideas and rivers of revelations. Just as everything upon the Earth can be paralleled to your soul, so can your soul be paralleled to universal systems beyond your wildest imagination. This fact is why you are able, if you so choose, to make your life a mindful journey rather than a burdened one, a delightfully connected mission rather than an isolated one, a creative adventure rather than a limited one. Never forget that *all of Life is esoteric*, for it is symbolic of the sacred, and can be recognized as such through extrapolation.

THE EXPERIMENTAL APPROACH

We are all the offspring of Divine Parents, forever learning, and therefore forever children at heart. Children need to play! And yet, at your approach to this creative process becomes laden with an unnecessary heaviness. Let us think for a moment what it would be like to approach spiritual service and development as play instead of work, to regard the methods we've discussed as toys, and to see the world as a kind of playground. Why not have fun with the principles you've been shown? They are given to bring joy and meaning, not to burden your heart with anxiety and guilt. Just as you look at your own children and want them to feel the sparkle of humor and the energy of enthusiasm in all that they do, so does your Team yearn for you to dance and skip as often as possible as you proceed through your journey. Rest assured, those on the Other Side make it a regular practice to do so!

One way to access this kind of carefree spiritedness is to look at life as a grand experiment. You rise each morning to a new lump of play dough that is waiting there for you to shape and mold. One of the characteristics of play dough is its pliability, and it's a good thing that this is so. If you start off with a dissatisfying shape, you aren't stuck — you are allowed to change it into something you like better. In fact, you are *invited* to do so! Take stock of the elements of your day from this standpoint, and see what happens. Look at the requirements of a particular day, and ask yourself, "Hmmm, what can I make out of all this? Where can I insert more joy? Where can I insert more fun? Where can insert more pleasure for others as well as myself? What could I do to surprise someone today? What could I do to uplift myself? What can I change about my intentions for today to align them more closely with play? And how can I share all this with others?"

Just by setting your thoughts on this course will, by divine default, cause all kinds of opportunities to arise whereby you may apply the experimental approach. There is a degree of non-attachment involved in this process. Instead of strong emotions and dramatic efforts, you will find that this approach asks you to minimize the intensity of emotions and react from an observational post. It is much like the difference between rushing to the side of a child who is having a temper tantrum and jumping into his game with an equivalent degree of hysteria or calmly maneuvering about the child with the intention of reducing the hysteria and perhaps even helping the child to see the foolishness of the moment by helping him laugh at himself. Therefore, while our ultimate goal is the abandonment of ourselves in spiritual play, the first step towards entering this state is nonattached observation.

Such non-attachment can be thought of as typical of a "spiritual scientist". As we know, scientists are curiously engaged in experimentation, and the first step in any experiment is to ask a question (in this case, "What can I do to bring more play into this moment?") before moving on to the observation phase. When you are observing, you are gathering data rather than formulating judgments or reacting. Once the observation has been made, and a plan of action is decided upon, we then have the chance to take that lump of play dough (i.e., our creation thus far) and see what we can make out of it. In other words, we now have a pre-planned reaction. Perhaps it is generalized, but at least it's planned, rather than impulsive.

If circumstances are nothing more than the culmination of certain vibrations coming together in manifestation, why not take the approach that we can change those vibrations, or if we are pleased with them, we can playfully maintain them as they are? The key to doing so is to feel them, observe them, be honest and clear on our alignment with them, and then to reach for a vibration slightly above the one we are in. This space between the one alignment and the next becomes our playground, the place we can begin to play with our creative power.

Energy is energy is energy, impartial and neutral, so all that is needed to elevate it is to shape it, increment by increment, step by step, a little closer to the desired point. Jumping in despair off the vibrational bridge of drama does nothing but plunge you into the very waters you are despairing about. Imagine standing on a bridge looking at a raging, swirling river and lamenting, "Look at that dark, murky river. I'm so disturbed by it, I'm going to jump right in it!" If you can instead just pause on that bridge and feel within yourself that inquisitive experimenter, that calm observer, and then observe that part of you that is observing, and then observe that observer of the observer… as far out as you can go, you will find yourself moving farther and farther away from the situation you are in.

As you elevate your perspective, you will see things as you do in an airplane during takeoff, and the big picture will become clearer. You will actually begin seeing things not simply through your earthly eyes but through the eyes of Team members who are positioned at certain points beyond you. In a sense, you will be joining your Team in their lookout towers. This will help you to formulate a reaction based upon the widest view you can possibly attain at that present moment. *Reacting from such a position is the essence of wisdom.*

Yes, there is wisdom in play! Look at the infinite wisdom of a child on the playground, who breaks the bonds of lethargy and runs with all her might across the grass, then enters into a world of fantasy where fairies live in flowers and wings grow on her back. How wise she is when she sloughs off any unhappy memories or reprimands of her little past and throws herself with abandon into a swing, pumping herself to greater heights of joy as she sings at the top of her lungs! How wise she is when she settles down beneath a tree and simply watches the other children for a while, learning from what she sees. And how wise she is when she jumps up and twirls about until she is dizzy, feeling what it's like to be in another dimension entirely. And then, how *exceedingly* wise she is when she lies on the bench and stares up at the treetops and sky above her and talks for a while with her imaginary friends.

Contrast this child with one who chooses to complain that he doesn't like that kind of swing, or it is too hot to play, or decides to disregard or even destroy the very things that have been placed there for the dual purpose of challenging him physically and bringing him pleasure. Indeed, you can learn volumes by watching a real playground full of children. There, you will see the ones who are out to find something negative to say as well as the ones who turn their playtime into a magical escapade. Same time, same place, same playground, same opportunity, regarded from two entirely different points of view. You, as an adult, are really no different. Your playground just has different equipment in it.

Of course, it is true that not only swings and blue skies greet you each day in your playground. But without fail, there is something in your playground that you can label as delightful. Even if it is but one thing, focus upon it, not briefly but with all the might you can muster, with all the appreciation and care you can feel, and you can be sure that the goodness you have reinforced will multiply. As we have said before, your thoughts go forth and connect with similar thoughts to form enormous spheres of energy that fuel more of the same. Therefore, your focus does not remain only yours. It is quickly taken up and multiplied again and again through the force of this sphere. If you can link up to these spheres deliberately and in a consistent manner, you will find yourself fueled with a strength that is beyond your own natural capacity to generate, for you'll be tapped into a source that is self-renewing, a source of which your Team is also a part.

Take a look at your playground of life… it is filled with sand which you may sculpt, toys with which you may pretend, swings on which you may soar, slides along which you may zoom, trees on which you may climb, friends whom you may love, and all the possible combinations of these things. If there are some things in the playground that are broken, you have access to a Team to help you fix them. The first step is to ask yourself, "What can I do with this set of playthings to make the best of this moment, this day, this phase of my life?" The answer *is* within you, and in that simple question you will discover the best way to bring a lighthearted approach into your experience. Remember, "This too shall pass" applies to both joy and pain, so why invest too fully in any of it? Play with it earnestly and sincerely, and be willing to move on.

It is said that a child's laughter is always just under the surface of their pout. Laughter is just under the surface of your soul as well, and the first step to that joyous discovery is to step back from the emotional swirls of temperament and simply observe — even if only for a brief moment — the elements that are available to you for shaping and molding. *Use your natural impulses of curiosity, creativity, and spiritual entrepreneurship,* as you assess what you can think, say, or do to insert a burst of playfulness, a current of creativity, a splash of "what else?" energy into any given situation. Acknowledge to yourself that you are experimenting with the principles you have learned for the purpose of seeing how much luster and sparkle you can add to your Now, and like an authentic spiritual scientist, watch the remarkable analysis, hypothesis, and final results unveil themselves. You are sure to be surprised, even astonished, at the power of play and joy to transform any vibration in your sphere of influence. Try it and see, right now, for Now is all you have!

TRUE JOY

What can one say about the essence of joy that is adequate to describe something more than mere humor, whimsical moments, or the passing pleasures of material life? I want you to know that there is a current of absolute joy flowing throughout the Universe, a river in a sense, a channel of rushing, bubbling beauty that you are always welcome to drink of, to float in, to launch your little boats of wonder upon. It is a channel that is not dependent upon circumstances or the actions of others. It is a channel that embraces all who enter it, and washes away all traces of cynicism and disbelief. If I had a "secret weapon" while I was upon the Earth through which I filtered everything, it was this stream of joy. And more than anything, I want all of you to have it.

True Joy is the result of living a life free of the burden of pride. It is a state of the heart that comes from no longer prioritizing your life around your looks, what you own, or if you are accepted or rejected by someone. For these are the things that lock you into activities that have no purpose whatsoever except to maintain those particular illusions. The energy it takes to keep those illusions propped up is exhausting, and causes a person to trudge about with additional pounds of distraction upon their shoulders.

True Joy comes with a peaceful resignation — not defeat but resignation — based upon the deep knowing that certain laws are at work in life, and there is no reason to run about being afraid of them or pretending to others that they do not apply to you. Think what makes a content child — one who knows and accepts the limits. Within this safety net, this child is now content to turn his energies towards things he is allowed to explore. The unhappy child is the one who is constantly banging his head against the gate that he is not permitted to open because he is simply not ready to explore beyond.

So it is with accepting the framework of the Universe. Once you do, you free that part of your mind that is scheming to break down the gate that is there for your own protection, the gate that you pridefully believe should not apply to you.

When you are no longer pushing to be something you are not, no longer rushing because you simply have no time left over for the honest and kind moments of life that create meaningful bonding, no longer grieving over the inevitable changes of the body that develop after time, no longer clinging to those things that must eventually deteriorate, no longer basing your sense of accomplishment upon your material surroundings, and no longer living in fear that you will be forsaken by someone, then you find yourself with a tremendous amount of extra emotional energy and an abundance of free spiritual time… time to meditate, time to wonder, time to play, time to converse, time to read, time to create, time to explore, time to minister to others, time to simply be. And this is True Joy.

The things that keep us from becoming fully immersed in this wonderful stream of joy are not things that are inherently "bad" in themselves. Used in moderation, all things can have value. But if these activities drive us to excess and rob us of the energy and time that rightfully belong to the soul and to valuable human interactions, we become lost in a sea of misplaced priorities. Suddenly, everything around us seems overwhelming. People are claiming that we are ignoring them. Our environment needs care. Our finances are in ruin. Yet, all the while we see ourselves as hard at work, running in circles, assuming that all this flurry of activity must yield good things in the end.

The truth is, the reason we are not producing fruit is because our priorities have become completely turned wrongside up! Instead of devoting adequate time to acknowledging the soul periodically throughout the day and then reaching out to our various responsibilities, we've reversed the structure, focusing on our material environment and giving the spiritual side of our natures barely a passing glance. Even more strange, instead of seeing our bodies as the useful tools that they are, we spend hours grieving over the absolutely unchangeable fact that they must deteriorate. This is tantamount to weeping because the sun is going down, as if our tears could change this fact somehow. All of these out-of-balance priorities rob us of True Joy and replace it with fear, a by-product of pride.

On the other hand, when priorities are in order, all the elements of our lives fall into place, and there is no flower in the garden that gets neglected-not our own selves, not our loved ones, not our friends, not our practical life. The knowledge that we belong to a Team and have a united mission should be the foundation of these priorities. Added to this foundation is the cultivation of a constant stream of spiritual communication first with God, then with those closest in your life, and then those on the periphery of your life.

Your physical environment — both the body and where you live and work — are next on this list, and the most successful way to tend to them is to create health and simplicity in your life *so that you are better able to ignore both the body and your surroundings.* If they are ailing, cluttered and uncared for, you will have to spend a great deal of time focusing on them, which will upset your proverbial apple cart. Prioritizing around the eternal verities of life translates into an efficiently managed life where *the body and its surroundings become more a vehicle for growth and less a distraction to your real purpose of being on the Earth.*

Envision your soul as the core that it is, and then consider what layers you will allow yourself to wrap around it. If you do not protect your time, energy, and activities from fragmented distractions, you will find your life to be a scattered mix of partial achievements, each of them characterized by confusion and

147

disappointment. I'm not suggesting a rigid schedule that is set because you are afraid of making a mistake. Joy is full of spontaneity and flexibility. But even that spontaneity can be directed toward things that add to the strength of your priorities, if you first become crystal clear about what those priorities are.

For example, if a businessman knows that his goal for the day is to get to a certain location, even a spontaneous decision to take the scenic route will factor in that ultimate goal to ensure that he arrives on time. The same approach can be taken with your daily decisions about what to do first and what should be saved for last. The person who places her connection to the Light first, and then sets goals that will increase the manifestation of that Light in her life and in the lives of those she knows is on the path to simplicity and joy. The person who regards physical abundance as something to appreciate and share rather than something to hoard in fear of losing it, is on the path to joy as well, for this person will not crumble in desperation when these physical treasures fade away, as they absolutely will, without exception.

If I could bottle one element I would be sure to put in the hands of all humanity, it would be that of Joy – the kind of joy that arises out alliance with that which is eternal — for it is the one thing that can carry you through any and all trials in life. It is so wonderful to see the humor in the path of life, even to see the potential of joy hidden in the painful experiences for there is a special kind of joy to be found there. It is the joy of the triumph, of the learning, of the wisdom gained! These lessons have be learned somewhere along the way, don't they? So how joyous it is that yet another lesson has been completed, mastered, and finished! How wonderful that it is no longer ahead of us, no longer something to fear. Rejoice, for it is over and done with, and we have that much more to teach others.

Oh, if we could all just laugh at ourselves more often, at our silly strivings to prop up things that cannot stay up, our futile efforts to pretend away those things that are staring us in the face. Try to choose laughing instead of crying whenever possible. Laugh at your own self as you laugh at a little child who is pouting and flaunting about over a cookie or such, because truly, many of your worries are of exactly that caliber, when viewed alongside the desperate needs and difficulties of so many other people in the world.

Free yourselves! Free yourselves of the heavy, stoic approach to "managing life" that causes you to limp from the weight of imaginary hardship. In most cases, simplifying your life and making less binding choices would remove most of your self-inflicted burdens, as would releasing attachments to the garment of the body. Come to know yourself first as a soul, and last as a body. *Indeed, come to identify the syllables of your very name with your soul,* and all your priorities will fall into place. Do this, and you will find yourself floating upon the surface of the stream of True Joy, propelled by a current of ease and naturalness while in the company of the most dynamic beings in the Universe – those who have chosen Joy as their North Star and compass!

THE GREAT TOOL OF OBSERVATION

One of the greatest tools we have is that of observation. In fact, it is best to spend more time in observation than in activity. This does not mean that we are not participants in life to the fullest. It only means that a part of us remains the observer of our thoughts, actions, and others' thoughts and actions, while seeking to discover the underlying dynamics of any circumstance in which we find ourselves. Great discoveries are found in the midst of situations when observation is used, for observation gives Life permission to speak to the deepest, calmest pool within your soul. It is an act of deliberate allowing, a clearing of a space so that wisdom may take root.

The tool of observation is as useful in the nonphysical realm as it is in the physical. There is so much to observe! Just as the physical realm includes countless and ever-changing number of grains of sand, so does the spiritual realm include countless and ever-changing bands of consciousness. Here, I visit various points of consciousness and dimensions that are not my habitual point for the purpose of observing how principles function on a lesser or grander scale, much like a senior student observes the juniors for review and the college students for inspiration. And in these visits, I find that no matter where one goes, the same principles are at work. Truly, "there is nothing new under the sun." The principles governing fire are the same for the insect as for the human, are they not? However, the abilities of the insect and the human to harness, flee or fight the fire (i.e., the consciousness) are like night and day. In the same way, the tool of observation "works" no, matter where one chooses to focus one's attention.

As mentioned before, I can visit many bands of consciousness like someone visits a certain neighborhood, and I am always cognizant of bands that are nearby. Entry into higher bands occurs by a type of vibrational invitation, and those invitations occur only when something can be accomplished by it. But wherever I may be, I am observing and learning.

You have perfect parallels upon the Earth. Does a toddler get to sit on the knee of a concert pianist and watch him play? Very rarely- and if it does happen, it is because there is a prior agreement on the spiritual plane that this inspirational experience would be made possible at an early age. A more common scenario is that of apprenticeship, where someone who is ready to be trained spends time in the mentor's environment. The concept of apprenticeship is an ancient one, and a direct reflection of the structure of the Team. Each of you has a mentor in the Team, a specific teacher assigned especially to you for this segment of your experience. Others are communicating with you as well, but this mentor is your main guide, and she may have many other apprentices with whom she works.

Observation is one of the main ways an apprentice learns from a mentor. Patiently watching, listening, asking pertinent questions, and not rejecting information that is at first difficult to accept is what accelerates understanding, whether the observation is of a spiritual or natural situation. Indeed, through observation, one learns to stop dividing experiences into "spiritual" or "physical," for they are nothing of the sort. *Everything is "spiritual" because everything is vibration at work* based upon Universal principles in action, with the Team in the middle of it all. Play with this concept in your life and see what happens. Revisit your environment, ask for the eyes of a child, and re-examine your surroundings from this position.

Even a few minutes of watching a butterfly flit from flower to flower can open a window of the soul. One day a month spent in silence can open a skylight to the heart. So often a seeker fills his/ her mind with constant stimulation and activity, but will not dedicate the smallest portion of their day to silence, reflection, or quiet observation Committing a portion of the day to observation and receptivity *and protecting that segment of time* is too valuable of a process to omit. To observe is to learn, and to apply what one has learned during observation is wisdom.

Choose silence over the constant insistence on speaking your mind. Choose to notice, but do not judge what you notice. You rarely know the complex background of any situation, so why spend useless energy on taking a stance about fragmented information? Observe how often you judge people on these fragmented impressions, and then notice how often you judge others for being judgmental! Choose to observe chaos without entering into the frenetic energy. Observe the less esteemed in a group and take time to acknowledge them, soul to soul. At times they are the most spiritually developed among you.

There are so many ways to practice observation. First is the practice of silence and meditation. Second is the practice of walking through one's day simply watching the activities of the world and the efforts of people to manage their lives, and noticing your own reaction to them. Third is the immersion of your attention in Nature, which is the most pure connection to the divine. Fourth is the observation of your own energy, words, and impulses in relation to a certain situation or individual. Fifth is to observe the least obvious element in a situation — the unnoticed item, person, angle of perspective, sound, and so forth. We habitually notice what everyone else is noticing, because focus can be quite contagious. Seek to break this pattern and notice what you would not normally see. By doing this in the natural, you help to awaken the same awareness in the spiritual. Remember, the Earth is a mirror to use in grooming yourself spiritually. If you do not take the time to observe, you will not see yourself or anything else clearly.

Observation can refresh and renew your Earth life experience, so that you come to embrace it with the eagerness of a child running into a playground. If you were presently in another dimension other than the Earth and were visiting various bands of consciousness, you might view the Earth and say, "Oh, there is a fascinating dimension in which to learn," for whatever dimension you are in, there are always others to consider. While upon the Earth, most people forget that they chose to go there for the great diversity of experiences that it offers both through observation and through hands-on participation. And while it is helpful to you to remain open to your teammates, it is not helpful to yearn to be elsewhere, to regard the Earth as some terrible dimension in which to exist. It is simply another vibratory field in which you are learning. It is pointless to constantly wish for "going to another dimension to learn and live in spiritual union." You *already are* in a dimension whereby you live and learn in union!

The grass is always greener, is it not? Please realize-you have so much beautiful green grass there on which to play. Embrace it with excitement and appreciation! Take time to notice the incredible wonders that are at work there, to see the challenges and pleasures of life as forces that you are learning to shape and direct. You can learn to walk through your days and be astounded again, like you were as a child, seeing a kitten for the first time, holding a crayon for the first time, swinging as you gaze up through the treetops for the first time! Imagine recapturing that feeling. Your Team knows that this is possible for you. Amazement and gratitude can be yours again once you learn to observe your precious Earth life as the treasure that it is, the incredible collection of vibratory manifestations that has welcomed you with open arms. Quiet your mind, open the amazing gifts of your senses, which are perfect reflections of your divine senses, and just observe. The beautiful school that you have chosen to attend will lead you to levels of extrapolation that you never thought possible, and you will know the true meaning of happiness.

CONNECTIONS

Throughout spiritual writings and popular philosophies of modern time, there is constant reference to a feeling of "connectedness". People refer to feeling connected to their own selves, or connected to the Universe while meditating or participating in certain activities. Society stresses this interconnectedness as the main tool for moving resources and expanding knowledge both in work and leisure.

I would like to broaden this concept of connections. Remember, you are not alone, and you are not really functioning as only "you". Your connection to your Team is real and tangible. It is not a dreamy idea of belonging to a secret, robed group of faceless beings. These souls are your dearest ones, as dear as the people you love so deeply on the Earth plane. You are sealed in promise to this Team. You belong. You have a place at the table that is only yours and cannot be filled by another. You are loved, understood, respected, and supported, and unlike some earthly relationships, your bond with them is eternal.

The majority of people do not allow themselves to feel much of this connection. Their consciousness is such that they perceive themselves as alone, even lonely, and in desperate need of fulfillment through the presence of others. I'm not saying that the urge to live within families and communities is anything less than normal and essential to human progress, but the idea that you are in any way abandoned if these human relationships end is the ultimate illusion. Indeed, all the impulses you have to build neighborhoods, or cluster together in social settings, or live in family units are based upon the beloved Team parallel above you. It is they that you "miss," and you transfer that emotion to your earthly life, a natural result of filtering divine principles through the flesh. And of course, a number of your Team members may be

154

right there with you, as family members, friends, colleagues, or as someone you have yet to encounter.

I am not in the least suggesting that you change your manner of living in these human units. These units are absolutely in divine order, and essential to your thriving. I am only saying that once the Team is real to you, your understanding of your most powerful emotions and impulses will become clearer, and this clarity, like all clarity, will yield liberation from dependency! It's not necessary to uproot or change any relationship structure in order to comprehend this teaching. If anything, it will enrich and strengthen all of your relationships. But knowing what is behind the emotions that drive you can transform your experience of those same emotions. Knowing your Team is your core connection to the joy and fulfillment you seek can bring a thrill to your life that wipes away loneliness and provides a steady stream of never-ending energy into all you do.

Realization of this can revolutionize your Earth life. As with all spiritual progress, change comes through the process of something becoming *real* to you. If your eyes could suddenly see the hosts that surround you, directing streams of divine information and fortified power into you, you would laugh with surprise and delight. Whether you ever develop such an enhanced sense of vision remains to be seen, but surely these revelations you now are receiving provide proof that an entire Team is working with you, with everyone, to the capacity you will *let* them.

Many claim that they are completely willing for the Team to establish this connection… that all the floodgates are open. But too often what is thought to be sincere is actually mere curiosity or hope for relief from pain. Most are not saying this because they want to live in the Truth, *whatever that takes and whatever that means.* "Living in the Truth" is an experience similar to the feeling you might have if you stood up in opposition against a crowd of racists who were taunting a man for the color of his skin-a feeling of righteous strength, of linking with the great leaders of the centuries who have walked before you, a feeling of passion, exhilaration, and absolute certainty of your position. You don't care if you have to stand in the cold rain as you make that proclamation — wild horses couldn't tear you away!

This unshakable devotion to discovering and channeling Truth is the direct line to your Team. As long as you are protecting any part of yourself from the all-revealing Light of Truth, your connection will contain areas that are shadowy and unlit. These areas are revealed to you gradually, as you increase your up-reach, and while not all will be considered "pleasant" by worldly standards, all will ultimately yield tremendous liberation, joy, and inner gifts that you have yet to tap. You cannot even visualize these things for the mere reason they are untapped, like oil yet undiscovered deep in the earth. "No eye has seen, nor ear heard, nor the heart of man imagined, what God has prepared for those who love him."

Therefore, cultivate your conscious awareness of your Team. Speak to them from the most authentic part of yourselves. Only goodness can possibly follow. Imagine sitting with a group of extremely wise and dear friends who want only the best for you, and asking for their honest opinion about something, asking that no words be spared. This is the experience of communing with your Team. In such a moment of communion, it is truly pointless to pretend anything whatsoever. Indeed, if you utter anything that is contrived, you will instantly hear your words repeated through their perspective and recognize the falseness for what it is. Be brave-ask that all falseness within your thoughts be revealed to you! They are working for your evolution and their evolution, knowing that all evolution ripples forth and influences every other point of consciousness. They are incapable of wanting anything but the highest good for you, for it is also their highest good. Your work is their work, your success is their success, and your growth is their growth. Social communities understand this principle when they proclaim, "Invest in our children, for they are our future." If earthly communities can see the importance of this, think how clearly spiritual teams perceive it.

Remember, the yearning for the connections you are working so hard to develop in your personal life has as its roots the soul's connection to its Team. Connection with them is the ultimate connection-seek it at every turn. The sense of unity, purpose, strength, and leadership that will result will free your life of fear, grief, loneliness, emotional or addictive dependencies, lack of confidence and doubt, while enriching all the relationships in your life. Now, just imagine that!

SUBCONSCIOUS ASSIGNMENTS

We all know what it feels like to forget a word or name only to have it jump into our awareness a few minutes, hours, or even days later. To our surprise, there it is, even though we'd stopped searching for it in our brains long ago. It's as if the brain had been given the task of scouring our memory banks to find that fragment of information while we went on to other things, and like a loyal assistant, it finally delivers, better late than never.

The tools that you have been given for realization and acceleration of growth can bring about this very same phenomenon within your spiritual nature. There is no more exciting way to live than being conscious that you are conscious, living with the knowledge that your consciousness is "on assignment" at all times, directing your life through inspiration and divine remembrance.

As said before, the goal is for one's spiritual impulses and intuitive guidance to become as automatic as are the involuntary systems of the heart and lungs. The way to initiate this process is to leave your consciousness some "directions" before you set forth each day to meet your earthly responsibilities. Request that the stream of insight, love and truth, which your Team is consistently and faithfully offering you, might enter the deepest recesses of your being, there to be absorbed into your essence. Ask for this searchlight to enter your most hidden parts, cleansing and refining your entire nature and illuminating your every decision.

Like the memory area of the brain that goes hunting for that missing word, ask that this light seek out the nooks and crannies of your being and reveal to you what you need to know in order to access greater wisdom. Have faith that even while the practicalities of life are upon you, your mind will be guided by your higher consciousness so that new and fresh information may rise to the surface of your awareness just when you need it the most. Proclaim that just as each of your organs automatically work their magic without any deliberate effort on your part, so will your consciousness stimulate, cleanse, and refine the inner workings of your being in an "automatic pilot" sort of way.

This process of auto-suggestion is similar to lucid dreaming, where the mind is primed before sleep to remain aware enough to influence one's dream midstream. Remember, you are a multi-dimensional being! Activating all aspects of your Self yields an in-pouring of light, much as the alignment of certain ancient monuments produces a burst of light through a carefully calibrated portal. It's a matter of lining up your vibratory condition on multiple levels with the intention of producing a beautiful, harmonious blend of energies. Just as the harmony of a song can lift the heart into ecstasy, so does *the harmony of one's inner vibrations lift one's being into communion with oneself and the Team.*

Again, vibrations are the result of one's intentions and motives, both conscious and subconscious. Be aware that people can have the same intention (such as, for example, opening a school) but their motives can be diametrically the opposite (seeking only profit, seeking to educate and nurture). Understanding your most elusive motives is key to establishing the purity of your intentions. Therefore, setting the course of both is crucial to attaining habitual consciousness on the seen and unseen dimensions. Here is a suggested prayer for lining up your intentions consciously, then leaving an "assignment" for your consciousness to continue on automatic pilot:

"I enter the flow of this day recognizing the gift of life upon the Earth and the opportunities it offers for growth and upliftment. My soul is united with my trusted Team, and I rest in the arms of that communion. While my earthly mind is focused on the tasks before me, I leave in place an emissary of thought, a representative of my higher will, to continue the process of inspiration and enlightenment. I know that when I most need this awareness, it will be

available to me. Answers will arise within me when I am confused, attributes of patience and leadership will arise within me when circumstances so require, and integrity will be the dominant quality in all my interactions, both in the seen and unseen dimensions. I embrace this process and the presence of my spiritual companions with utmost gratefulness, and join them in making this period of time on Earth a reflection of our highest mutual creation."

THE GOLD AND SILVER OF IT ALL

I invite you now to consider the principle of Gender as it manifests on the Earth and throughout the Universe. To maintain the broadest perspective possible, I ask you to drop any notion of male and female and replace it with the notion of two grand forces, Force Silver and Force Gold. Gold alternates primarily between stillness (ideation) and initiating (creating), and Silver alternates primarily between receiving (manifestation) and duplication (reflecting). I use the word "primarily" because both forces are capable of both roles, but primarily function as one or the other. Notice that both of these roles have phases of rest and motion.

The Universe is created from, sustained by, and developed through the principle of Gender. Indeed, if there is ever to be the recognition of one unifying and primary principle, it will be this one, for there is nothing that does not contain these two forces, absolutely nothing. According to the scientific "rule of eight," within every atom we can observe the natural desire of the atom to complete the pattern of each of its rings with a specific number of particles of energy (electrons = silver, protons = gold). It is this search for fulfillment that causes an atom to "fill out its rings" by "borrowing" electrons from neighboring atoms. In this way, the atom is made complete and has the capacity to manifest its true nature; in other words, to become the kind of atom it is destined to be. Learn the rule of eight and you have learned the meaning of spiritual gender, the rule of eternity.

Just as *scientific theory* proves the tendency in Nature towards union, *spiritual theory* proves that the soul is endowed with the same tendency. Each soul contains both forces of Gold and Silver, just as every baby has both testosterone and progesterone in their chemistry. Therefore, the soul unites with Earth bodies of either gender to learn the full scope of human knowledge, but retains identification with its primary alliance.

Forget your current gender, or how feminine or masculine you appear in your life, as you ponder your own alliance with Silver or Gold. *The value of your body's gender lies in the experiences it provides you.* Your body's gender does not determine, limit, or define you. In your essential state, you are a glorious mix of the two, yet maintain a primary alliance which enables you to participate in what might be regarded as the Divine Marriage.

Babies are born from physical union. Souls are born from spiritual union. Therefore, you have a Spiritual Mother and Father, who have spiritual parents, who have spiritual parents, who have spiritual parents… on into eternity. "In the beginning was the Word, and the Word was with God, and the Word was God." Before a word can be spoken, it must be ideated. Gold ideates, Silver manifests; thus do we have Creation. "Let us make man in our image. Male and female created He them." Everything in the Universe is done in pairs, from the pollination of a flower to the creation of a star. Your spiritual parents created you through the union of highly refined forces. You are the children of divine beings united at the most divine level, and these divine beings are the children of other divine beings.

The Will aspect of your spiritual body, if it were made visible to the human eye, is both silver and gold. Notice the balance of restraint or stillness that you instinctively utilize when you are applying your will to a situation. This is due to the two forces at play within that lightning bolt of power. The balancing of your own Silver and Gold forces prepares you to unite with your partner and to "give birth" to a spiritual child. The creation of this child is the first creative step of the balanced soul when it completes its earthly commitments. We see the parallel in some human families, where couples marry, prepare their life to receive a new addition, and then create or adopt a child. Following this event is a phase whereby more and more creativity occurs, from the enlargement of the family's home to the addition of playground equipment in the yard to the purchasing of a second car. This is a phase of envisioning possibilities and manifesting them for the good of the family. So it is with one's spiritual bonding. A new soul is birthed from the union of the two spiritually mature souls, followed by a phase of envisioning (which is the ideation) of incredible possibilities, which are sent forth to be manifested in various dimensions.

These ideations or "inventions" are created at the highest level, with the intention that they will be utilized in the most peaceful and environmentally caring manner. Everything that has been invented on the Earth for the betterment of the human experience has been first created in the realm of ideation between these pairs. Any other use of them is due to a distortion of interpretation as the ideas pass through the filter that surrounds the Earth. The vision of these inventions radiate out through the Universe and are magnetically collected on many dimensions. They are then interpreted through the bands of consciousness there, resulting in a myriad of manifestations.

Earth minds gather this information and interpret it in one manner, while those in other dimensions gather the same information and mold it according to their understanding. The same ideation appears in many different forms from one dimension to the next. For example, nuclear power, which is the ideation of a Team, is being translated differently in other dimensions than how it is being translated on Earth. Even on the Earth, you see differing uses for it-some peaceful and some violent. Imagine how unique the uses are elsewhere!

The variety in the uses of a given ideation is no different from the variety you would find if ten people were handed a wheel and told to think of things to do with it. One might use it on a cart, another might use it on a pulley, while another might paint it and use it as a decoration. Ingenuity is found in every dimension, for it is intrinsic to the creative urge. Inventions are only one example of what is created by these paired souls. The creations range from the practical to the infinitely complex. Some pairs within the most elevated bands of consciousness create new galaxies!

The forces of Gold and Silver in the creative process are so essential that we cannot adequately describe them. In other words, they cannot be isolated or objectified, for they are embedded in every breath of the Universe. Rest assured that your destiny is to be wholly united at the spiritually cellular and Universal levels. In truth, you already move and live and have your being in this state of unity; all appearances to the contrary are simply due to your perception. Remember the analogy of the baby that is sitting in front of the painting. Every component of the painting is there before her, fully available, but she is not conscious of it — at least not yet! One day, she will look at the painting and suddenly know what it is. She will have no idea how she knows, or when she had the capacity to know, but there it will be, clear as day. You have the ability to attain such clarity, too. Indeed, it is your destiny!

The Silver and the Gold that lies within and without you, the partnering from which you sprang, the partnering that is your destiny, the partnering of the Team, and the partnering that is producing all that you can see and imagine *is* the Divine Reality. For this reason do we stress again and again: *You are not alone. You are not really even functioning as one person. Nobody is. You are members of a Team, a spiritual Team that is closer to you than breathing.* Therefore, be at peace. Take refuge in the net of the spiritual principles that hold you in their care. Rejoice in the knowledge that you are connected in every way to your Team and to those you love who reside in other dimensions. *Appreciate the dimension you are in.* It is a wonderland of opportunity. Open your inner eyes and see those around you for who they really are . . . souls grouped in Teams seeking exactly what you are seeking. Strive to see the hodgepodge that is the Earth for what it really is — symbols of various points of consciousness, markers on the Earth that represent the creative force of human ingenuity passed through the Earth's filter. Take responsibility for these markers, for you have left many of them behind yourself. Understand that your urge to create more refined markers comes from your spiritual desire to compensate for your participation in the making of the other ones. Know that you have the power to cleanse your perceived past, for Light reaches the deepest recesses of our being, and enlightenment is *retroactive* and condenses everything into the vibrational now.

Release any disappointment in what appears to be failed attempts in life. Know that everything you have ever sent forth from the place of purest intention exists and thrives on another plane. Realize that there is nothing lost, and that you are much vaster than you think, for you are not wholly invested in one dimension. Believe in your own innate nature which includes Love, Will and Grace through Legacy. Call out to your spiritual ancestry, and honor the nobility of that legacy as it creates a direct line to the pairs and teams that stretch eternally beyond you.

Remember that you have the ability to experience the smallest moment on Earth and extrapolate it out to embrace the farthest reaches of your awareness. And remember that consciousness is the only reality, now is the only time, and observation is your greatest tool to function in this now. Most of all, remember that all of you are loved in a most powerful and everlasting way, that you are valued, watched over and guided beyond your grandest comprehension. You are children of divine beings, and destined to blossom as the same. There is so much to be joyful about-let this joy be your cornerstone, filling you with contentment, for you are all upon the path of ever-expanding consciousness.

WHO ARE TEDDY AND FRANCES KEY?

In the early hours of June 16, 1924, a baby girl named Crystal Nance Trager was born in Albury, Australia to Ann Mahoney and Frank Trager. She was their second daughter, and as time unfolded, it became clear that her destiny would include many gifts: an almost legendary talent in singing, a natural way of teaching and guiding children, and an unquenchable yearning for the meaning of life and communion with God. Her parents raised her as a Catholic, and after her christening and confirmation names were added, the little girl possessed the unwieldy name of Gloria Crystal Nance Mary Magdalene Trager. They called her "Teddy".

By the time she was nineteen, Teddy was living in the USA, one of many war brides who had immigrated during WWII. Her Texas-born husband, Raymond Key, remained in the Pacific while she stayed with her in-laws until the war ended. Teddy eagerly anticipated starting a family, envisioning a houseful of many children. Little did she know that her dream would come true, but not quite the way she'd imagined. She had two daughters of her own. Frances Rae was born in 1952, and Kelly Elizabeth arrived thirteen years later.

Teddy didn't want to leave her children while she worked, so she established a private school and day care center attached to her home in Jacksonville, Florida. She also continued her quest for truth. Her Catholic upbringing had left her with too many unanswered questions, and she realized she wanted a different kind of spiritual instruction for her children. When Frances, ho she'd nicknamed "Frankie," turned five, she left the church of her childhood. It took bravery to break from tradition, but she had always been an adventurer. She began to search out new avenues of faith by visiting various churches, Frankie in hand.

Frankie and Teddy were quite inseparable. Frankie had grown up in her mother's day care and school and was accustomed to being with her most of the time. Teddy understood Frankie's sensitive nature, and cultivated her daughter's love of music and reading, recognizing that Frankie had an unusual ability with the written word. Like her mother, Frankie could read at the age of three. She read and wrote well-crafted stories and poems of an insightful nature starting at the age of eight. By the age of ten, she was presenting her poetry at the Unitarian Church, where Teddy had found a haven, and was included in some of their spiritual discussion groups.

One of the evening groups delved into the subjects of the afterlife, spirit communication, and similar topics. When the matter of automatic writing was brought up, Frankie said, "I can do that." She described how sometimes when she wrote her "spiritual poems" she felt like she was being divinely guided with the words.

The group decided to try it out, right there and then, and put a pencil in her hand and a blindfold over her eyes. They played meditative music, and Frankie began to write. The words were linked together as one long word, and people began to ask questions. Frankie's hand would answer them in words and concepts far beyond her ten years.

Only one excerpt of these writings has remained through the years, which reads: *"Once as a person wanders through a corridor of Thought, he shall prove himself as an animal with a being only as a halo can imagine. Perfectness: Once a healer will touch you and create a world apart from your physical contents, to cleanse your fullness from a content undesirable. Contact us, often and make it a love, to create a new light for you that is meaningful. Love from the goodness of my heart…"*

Below: Frankie, at age 10, the time of the automatic writing

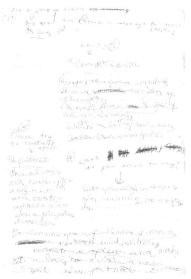

These sessions continued for some months until other interests took over. Teddy began to read "Mysticism" by Evelyn Underhill, an analysis of the mystical life as viewed primarily from the esoteric Christian perspective, and she discarded other activities such as hypnotism, Oujia boards, and automatic writing, believing there was a higher, more direct manner of communing with the Divine. Frankie's spiritual interest shifted with her mother's and by the time she was twelve, they were both attending The Universal Church of Ontology in Jacksonville, Florida, a beautiful little chapel that used Christian vernacular, music, and atmosphere to present mystical teachings.

For about fifteen years, they remained in this church, becoming ordained ministers and singing in the choir as well as writing and delivering sermons. Teddy's exquisite voice was a powerful and beloved treasure for the small congregation and she was the main soloist, often moving people to tears with the warm, healing quality of her songs. In 1978, Teddy left the Church, disillusioned with the interpersonal issues that inevitably come up in such small groups, and Frankie did the same a year later. The church relocated to North Carolina.

Teddy established a second private school on a beautiful ten-acre piece of land filled with oak trees that she called "Summerhill". There, she built a home for herself and Kelly to live in. Frankie and her children lived behind the school, and for a short while they formed a little church of their own. They maintained vegetable and flower gardens and had a number of animals for the children to enjoy. Teddy, her friends and other family members continued to meet and share spiritual insights. She remained a leader among her peers, an invigorator for exploration into deeper wisdom. Most importantly, though, she applied these spiritual principles to her dealings with humanity, particularly with the children she taught. As a result, she was adored by the teens she took into her school, many who were floundering due to personal and family difficulties.

Throughout the years, she was described by many of these young people as being the person who saved them from despair, the one who kept them afloat, who believed in them, sheltered them and salvaged them from emotional and moral quagmires. She was a rock and haven for these youth, and her home was open to them day and night.

When she turned sixty, Teddy closed her school and became a housemother at a runaway shelter for teens, where she again applied her philosophy of "seeing the Christ in everyone" to the troubled youth she met. As time went by, she took into her home a variety of people who others had rejected, including refugees, homeless people, and people just down on their luck.

Her own children and grandchildren remained her focus, however, and she showered them with her affection, spunky humor, and assistance in every way she possibly could. There was no error that she did not forgive, and the concept of holding a grudge was nonexistent to her. Her family lived in awe of this inspiring, unassuming woman in their midst who often said to them, "I feel like I am part of a Team. Some of us are here, and some of us are over there." And while she was open to the many paths through which people seek enlightenment, she would claim, "If we could all live the teachings of Jesus, the world would be a perfect place."

Frankie lived in a variety of places, but in the end, she returned to live with her mother on the property, where they continued to experience remarkable spiritual events together. One of such events in the 1990s involved the appearance of an angelic apparition in Teddy's room. Frankie was asleep on the floor of her mother's room because her mother had undergone some surgery. During the night, her mother began to talk in her sleep about a "Sister". Her talking awakened Frankie who lay listening to Teddy for a while, and then a brilliant flash of light filled the room. Stunned by the light, they both sat up immediately, and Teddy described that while she was asleep she had a vision of a nun named Sister Theresa who was teaching her about Divine Love. Frankie turned on the lamp, and there on the floor between Teddy's bed and Frankie's blankets was the imprint of two small human footprints, deeply embedded in the carpet as if they'd been permanently impressed there by the manufacturing company.

They examined the footprints closely and found that they were unable to remove them by brushing or vacuuming. These footprints remained firmly imprinted on the carpet for many months to come. This was just one of many such incidences that Teddy and Frankie shared; numerous members of her family and circle of friends can recount similar experiences they experienced with Teddy as well.

As Teddy grew older, her family encouraged her to write down her life story and spiritual perspectives, even offering to help her. Teddy started to do so upon several occasions, but seemed unable to maintain the project. She would, in turn, tell Frankie, "You should try doing that automatic writing like you used to do as a little girl," but Frankie would claim she had no interest in it, and in fact was a little afraid of stories she'd heard of such activities attracting mischievous spirits. Back and forth they would go about this topic, and in the end neither pursued their writing.

In April of 2008, it was discovered that Teddy had cancer. Chemo and radiation followed, and she rallied enough to see a musical that Frankie had written about Teddy's life, which was performed at a local theatre. "Aussie Song" was embraced wholeheartedly by both by the cast and the community, for it captured the magic of Teddy's early years in Australia, her close bond with her father, and her immigration to America. The Universe had timed it perfectly, allowing Teddy, her family, her dearest friend Vivien and her sister Merle to share the experience together, not only once, but throughout nine shows!

Family and friends cared for Teddy as her illness progressed until October 9, 2010, when Teddy passed away at "Summerhill," the acreage she had always loved so dearly. Looking back, Frankie knows now that the sensation she felt at the moment of her mother's passing was some kind of an "exchange of spiritual DNA" between the two of them. It seemed that some part of Teddy remained in Frankie, and some part of Frankie departed with her mother, enabling what was to follow.

At her memorial, a large gathering of people came to express the impact that Teddy had made on their lives with her generosity of spirit, resources, and heart. One man summed it up when he said, "I came to Teddy a broken boy. I had been thrown away like a piece of trash. She took me in and she loved me, taught me I was worth something. She truly saved my life." It appears that Teddy is still expressing that love to humanity. Just as Frankie and Teddy had encouraged one another to do, both are now writing again. Teddy has found in Frankie a channel to express her broader scope of wisdom, and Frankie is not afraid to open herself to the process of inspirational writing, fully confident of the integrity of her contact. Those who know Teddy recognize her voice in this work, and are grateful beyond words that she is still with them, continuing to enlighten their walk through life.

ADDENDUM

Moments before I was to send the files of this book to the printing company, my cousin Lisa Peeler sent me an email. She had met someone named Shoumen from India who was devoted to Mother Teresa and carried in his wallet a card signed by her own hand. Teddy was an avid admirer of the work and writings of Mother Teresa, and would often quote her, saying, "I pray only to be a pencil in His hand." A photocopy of the card was attached to the email that read:

Dear Shoumen

**The fruit of Silence is Prayer
The fruit of Prayer is Faith
The fruit of Faith is Love
The fruit of Love is Service**

God bless you

Mc Teresa m c.

MOTHER TERESA

I was profoundly struck by the timing of the arrival of such a message, and felt it to be a blessing from God, Mother and her Team upon this book. To me, it's an acknowledgement of the gift we have received in these writings, but also reminds me that all that has been written in these pages can be encapsulated in these few words of Mother Teresa, who so purely embodied the simplicity of the spiritual path . . . Prayer, Faith, Love, and Service.

Heartfelt thanks
for the practical assistance and
spiritual support of these dear ones
in the production of this book:

Lisa Peeler
Alan Curran
Barbara Andridge
Kelly Key
Leslie Shapero
Cheryl Comer
Carla Hodge
Darrell McNeil

And to the many unseen hearts, minds
and souls who have contributed to this
message both here and from the Other Side.

**To order books or contact Frances Key
directly, visit: www.TheTeamBooks.com**

23610586R00106

Printed in Poland
by Amazon Fulfillment
Poland Sp. z o.o., Wrocław